BIODIVERSITY CONSERVATION AND SUSTAINABLE DEVELOPMENT

एडमंड को 'ऑर्डर ऑफ न्यूजीलैंड' की सदस्यता प्रदान की गई।

1989

पीटर मूलग्रियू की विधवा जून से एडमंड ने शादी की।

1990

एडमंड के पुत्र पीटर सफलतापूर्वक एवरेस्ट की चोटी तक पहुँचे।

1999

'ए व्यू फ्रॉम द समीट' पुस्तक का प्रकाशन हुआ।

2002

सर एडमंड के हिमालयन ट्रस्ट का नियंत्रण शेरपाओं के हाथों में सौंपा गया।

2008

11 जनवरी को ऑकलैंड में सर एडमंड हिलेरी का देहांत हो गया।

□

संदर्भ ग्रंथ

1. हाई एडवेंचर : एडमंड हिलेरी
2. सर एडमंड हिलेरी : सैम्युअल विलार्ड कॉम्पटोन
3. सर एडमंड हिलेरी एंड द पीपुल ऑफ एवरेस्ट : सिंकिया रूस रामसे
4. सर एडमंड हिलेरी एन एक्स्ट्रा ऑर्डिनरी लाइफ : एलेक्सा जॉनसन
5. सर एडमंड हिलेरी : मॉडर्न डे एक्सप्वोरा : क्रिस्टिन ब्रेनन
6. टीचिंग द समिट : सर एडमंड हिलेरीज स्टोरी : एलेक्सा जॉनसन, डेविड लार्सेन
7. एडमंड हिलेरी : फर्स्ट टू द टॉप : डेन एलीश

BIODIVERSITY CONSERVATION AND SUSTAINABLE DEVELOPMENT

By

Dr. Rajib Lochan Panigrahy

&

Dr. Lingaraj Patro

DISCOVERY PUBLISHING HOUSE PVT. LTD.

NEW DELHI-110 002

First Published-2008

ISBN 978-81-8356-333-8

Published by:

DISCOVERY PUBLISHING HOUSE PVT. LTD.
4831/24, Ansari Road, Prahlad Street,
Darya Ganj, New Delhi-110002 (India)
Phone: 23279245 • Fax: 91-11-23253475
E-mail: dphbooks@rediffmail.com
dphtemp@indiatimes.com
Website: www.discoverypublishinghouse.com

Printed at:
Arora Enterprises
Laxmi Nagar, Delhi–110 092

Preface

Since, civilization built till now the human activities are rapidly going on with the rapid growth of population for fulfilling the human needs in day-to-day life to comfort and luxury which is utilizing the natural resources. The rapid use of natural resources without requiping any creates ecological imbalance which causes pollution of different types what causes disasters of natural and man-made which are creating deterioration of environment courses threat to the living organisms on the globe. In the drastic ecological imbalance and pollution day-by-day the creatures, plants (i.e. flora and fauna in botanical terms) extincting from the earth. With the living organs, trees and plants existence not only man survive but also they can. Hence, for all the living organisms, Bio-diversity become an alarming danger because all are co-related with each other as the world is a family, they are members of the family living in.

Hence, people should be more a ware and alert about the preservation of environment and protection of flora & fauna on the earth to live in healthy and wealthy atmosphere with sufficiency of resources.

The paper contributors have narrated on the topic elaborately on their research eminence with special care to make the book worthy and the publisher by kind enough to publish it.

• **Authors**

Contents

Contents

1

BIODIVERSITY CONSERVATION AND SUSTAINABLE DEVELOPMENT

*S.K. Palita**

Introduction

Biological diversity, or *biodiversity*, is a term used to describe the great variety of life on Earth. The Convention on Biological Diversity defines it as "...the variability among living organisms from all sources including *inter alia,* terrestrial, marine and other aquatic ecosystems and the ecological complexes of which they are a part; this includes diversity within species, between species and of ecosystems". In other words, plants, animals and micro-organisms, their genes, and the ecosystems that living organisms inhabit, are all facets of biodiversity (IUCN, 2002).

Conservation and sustainable use of biodiversity is fundamental to ecologically sustainable development. Biodiversity is part of our daily lives and livelihood, and constitutes resources upon which families, communities, nations and future generations depend. Every country has the responsibility to conserve, restore and sustainably use the biological diversity within its jurisdiction. Biological diversity is fundamental to the fulfillment of human needs. An environment rich in biological diversity offers the broadest array of options for sustainable economic activity, for sustaining human welfare and for adapting to change.

India—A Land of Megadiversity

India is one of the 12 mega biodiversity countries in the world. India's wide range of climatic and topographical features has resulted in a high level of ecosystem diversity encompassing forests, wetlands, grasslands, deserts, coastal and marine ecosystems, each with a unique assemblage of species.

* Department of Zoology, Nayagarh Autonomous College, Nayagarh—752069, Orissa.

India has a rich and varied heritage of biodiversity covering ten biogeographical zones, the trans-Himalayan. the Himalayan, the Indian desert, the semi-arid zone(s), the Western Ghats, the Deccan Peninsula, the Gangetic Plain, North-East India, and the islands and coasts (Rodgers, Panwar and Mathur; 2000).

The forests cover an actual area of 63.73 million ha (19.39 per cent) and consist of 37.74 million ha of dense forests. 25.51 million ha of open forests and 0.487 million ha of mangroves, apart from 5.19 million ha of scrub, comprise 16 major forest groups. These range from the tropical wet evergreen forests in the northeast to the sub-alpine and alpine forests of the Himalayas through the tropical dry deciduous and tropical thorn forests of Central and Western India. Wetlands include a rich diversity of inland and coastal wetland habitats covering 4.1 million ha of the landmass. A number of rare and threatened species of plants and animals including *Aldrovanda vesiculosa, Utricularia minor, Cervus eldii eldii (Manipur brow-antlered deer), Cervns duvaucelli (swamp deer),* and *Lepidochelys olivacea (Olive Ridley turtle)* are associated with wetland habitats.

The coastline of India extends over 7,500 km while the marine ecosystems cover 2.1 million sq. km (MoEF, 1999). The under-explored marine world contributes 15 per cent of the total faunal biodiversity of the country. India has some of the most unique mangrove swamps in the world, in the alluvial deltas of the Ganga, Mahanadi, Godavari, Krishna and Cauvery rivers and the Andaman and Nicobar islands, while coral reefs, considered the most productive marine ecosystems, occur in the Andaman and Nicobar islands, Lakshwadeep. and the Gulfs of Kutch and Mannar.

Deserts cover 2 per cent of the Indian landmass and include the sandy Thar desert of Western Rajasthan and adjoining states, the salt desert of Kutch and the high altitude cold deserts of Jammu and Kashmir and Himachal Pradesh.

Surveys conducted so far in India have inventoried over 47,000 species of plants and over 89,000 species of animals over just 70 per cent of the country's total area (MoEF, 1999). India's biogeographical location at the junction of the Agro-tropical,

Indo-Malayan and Paleo-Arctic realms has contributed to the biological richness of the country. A total of 89,451 animal species has been recorded in India accounting for 7.31 per cent of the faunal species in the world (MoEF, 1999).

The endemism of Indian biodiversity is high—about 33 per cent of the country's recorded flora is endemic to the country and is concentrated mainly in the North-East, Western Ghats, North-West Himalaya and the Andaman and Nicobar islands. About 62 per cent of the known amphibian species and 50 per cent of the lizards are endemic to India, the majority occurring in the Western Ghats (MoEF, 1999).

India supports 15,000 species of flowering plants, 5,000 of them exclusive to us. Out of 317 species of mammals in India, 38 of them are endemic. Out of 969 species of birds in India, 69 of them are endemic. India has 389 species of reptiles, 156 exclusive to us. Similarly, out of 206 amphibians found in India, 110 are endemic. In the matters of biodiversity, India stands closer to tenth in the pecking order of nations in the wealth of the total number of living species (Gadgil, 2005).

The National Bureau of Plant Genetic Resources has over 1,59,080 varieties and 1,07,018 germplasm collections. Much of the country's agrobiodiversity is in the custody of farming communities/tribals who followed age-old farming systems. Genetic diversity comprising native species and landraces is concentrated in the areas of the Western Ghats, north-eastern Himalayas, southern plateau, central India and north-western Himalayas. Wild relatives of wheat and barley are located in the western and north-eastern Himalaya while a major centre for wild rice is the eastern-peninsular India. Domesticated livestock and poultry include 27 breeds of cattle, 8 breeds of buffalo, over 42 breeds of sheep, 20 breeds of goats, 7 breeds of camel. 8 breeds of horses, and a few types of pigs. Of about 20,000 species comprising the fish genetic resources of the world, nearly 11 per cent (or 2118 fish species) have been reported in India, including the finfishes from the Western and Eastern Ghats (MoEF, 2001).

This immense diversity has resulted in the inclusion of two Indian regions in the 25 global biodiversity hotspots. These

2 hotspots, the Western Ghats/Sri Lanka and the Indo-Burma region (covering the Eastern Himalayas) encompassing parts of India and adjoining countries are amongst the top eight most important hotspots (Myers, Mittermeier, Mittermeier *et al.*, 2000):

As many as 14 ecoregions lying completely or in part within India figure amongst the Global 200, which are outstanding examples of the world's diverse ecosystems based on criteria such as species richness, species endemism, unique higher taxa, unusual ecological or evolutionary phenomena, and global rarity of major habitat types. The Indian ecoregions are the Chhota-Nagpur Dry Forests, Eastern Dcccan Plateau Moist Forests, Eastern Himalayan Alpine Meadows, Eastern Himalayan Broadleaf and Conifer Forests. Indus river delta, Maldives, Chagos, Lakshwadeep Atolls, NagaManipuri-Chin Hills Moist Forests, Rann of Kutch Flooded Grasslands, South-western Ghats Moist Forests, Sunderbans Mangroves, Terai-Duar Savannas and Grasslands, Tibetan Plateau Steppe, Western Ghats Rivers and Streams, Western Himalayan Temperate Forests (Olson and Dinerstein, 1998). India accounts for 6 per cent of the total number of ecoregions.

The country is also one of the 12 primary centres of origin of cultivated plants and domesticated animals. It is considered to be the homeland of 167 important plant species of cereals, millets, fruits, condiments, vegetables, pulses, fibre crops and oil seeds and 114 breeds of domesticated animals. India stands quite high in the wealth of total number of living species.

Biodiversity *vis-a-vis* Cultural Diversity

This biological diversity is reflected in the cultural diversity of the people whose very existence is tied to the continued maintenance and sustainable use of biological resources. India has a rich ethos of biodiversity-conservation and traditional knowledge systems and it is these practices that have given rise to informal and localised *in situ* conservation. Traditional farming practices are directly responsible for the country's treasure trove of agro-diversity. The multidimensional cultures of India have protected biodiversity by using indigenous knowledge system. Traditional systems like Ayurveda, Siddha,

Unani are dependent on medicinal plant sources and have, in turn, helped maintain their diversity as well.

The Value of Biodiversity

The well-being and survival of human populations are dependent on millions of species of plants, animals and microbes. These include species and varieties of crops, livestock and wildlife. Biodiversity has numerous values in agriculture, medicine, food and industry. Biodiversity maintains ecological balance and evolutionary processes, and has spiritual, cultural, aesthetic and recreational values. The ecosystem services rendered include pollination, chemical recycling, nutrient cycling, soil maintenance and climatic regulation. For example, by absorbing huge volumes of atmospheric carbon dioxide, forests regulate global climate and slow the effect of global warming. Wetlands such as lakes and marshes regulate flow of water and help prevent flooding.

Loss of biodiversity has serious economic and social costs for any country. The experience of the past few decades has shown that as industrialisation and economic development in the classical sense takes place, patterns of consumption, production and needs, change, straining, altering and even destroying ecosystems. India, a megabiodiversity country, while following the path of development, has been sensitive to needs of conservation and hence is still rich in biological resources. Ethos of conservation and harmonious living with nature is very much ingrained in the lifestyles of India's people.

Biodiversity : Uses

All forms of life—plants, animals and humans—are so clearly interlinked that any disturbance in one gives rise to imbalance in the other. All life on earth is inter-dependent and man is only a strand in this delicate web of relationship. Our own species is subjected to evolutionary processes as any other life. The greater the diversity of wild species, the greater is the opportunity for production of new species; the greater is the opportunity for production of new varieties. Almost all crops and livestock on which we depend upon for food production are hybrids, the result of cross breeding, originally from wild species. Hybrids species are vulnerable to an epidemic or any abnormal climatic variation, compared to their wild ancestor, which kill them. Without the wild ancestor, it might not be possible to replace them. Wildlife act as "Biological indicators", *i.e.,* they warn us about any potentially dangerous change as they are highly sensitive to any environmental changes. The medicinal utilities of a variety of species are yet to be identified. The greater the variety of wildlife we conserve, the more we will be able to learn from them.

THREAT TO BIODIVERSITY

Threatened Species

Despite the many measures taken for the protection, conservation and sustainable use of biodiversity, many species and ecosystems are seriously threatened. The 2000 IUCN Red List of Threatened Species (IUCN, 2000) is provided in Tables 1.1 and 1.2.

According to the Red List of Threatened Animals (IUCN, 2000), 44 plant species are critically endangered, 113 endangered and 87 vulnerable. Amongst animals, 18 are critically endangered, 54 endangered and 143 are vulnerable. Ten species are Lower Risk conservation dependent, while 99 are Lower Risk near threatened. India ranks second in terms of the number of threatened mammals, while India is sixth in terms of countries with the most threatened birds (IUCN, 2000).

Table 1.1 Threatened species of India

Taxonomic group	*Number of threatened species*
Mammals	86
Birds	70
Reptiles	25
Amphibians	3
Fish	3
Molluscs	2
Other Invertebrates	21
Plants	244
Total	**459**

Source: IUCN (2000). Red list of threatened animals. IUCN. Gland, Switzerland

Table 1.2 Threatened plants and animals of India by status category

	Ex	*EW*	*CR*	*EN*	*VU*	*LR/cd*	*LR/nt.*	*DD*
Plants	7	2	44	113	87	1	72	14
Animals	0	0	18	54	143	10	99	31

Legend. EX-extinct; EW-Extinct in the Wild; CR-Critically Endangered; VU-Vulnerable; LR/cd-Lower risk conservation dependent; LR/NT = Lower risk near threatened.

Source: IUCN (2000), Red list of threatened animals. IUCN. Gland, Switzerland

Causes of Loss of Biodiversity

"As human population has surged this century, the population of numerous other species have tumbled, many to the point of extinction. Indeed, we live amid the greatest extinction of plant and animal life since the dinosaurs disappeared some 65 million years ago, which species losses at 100 to 1,000 times the natural rate. But humans are not just witnesses to a rare historic event, we are actually its cause. The leading sources of today's species loss, habitat alteration, invasions by exotic species, pollution, and overhunting are all a function of human activities (Lakshmi Narasaiah, 2005).

Human activities have pushed the per centage of mammals, amphibians, land fish that are in "immediate danger" of extinction into double digits. The principal cause of species extinction is habitat loss—the result of encroachment by humans for settlements, for agriculture, or to claim resources such as timber. A particularly productive but vulnerable habitat is found in coastal areas, home to 60 per cent of the world's population. Coastal wetlands nurture two thirds of all commercially caught fish, for example. And coral reefs have the second highest concentration of biodiversity in the world, after tropical rainforest. But human encroachment and pollution are degrading these areas: roughly half of the world's salt marshes and mangrove swamps have been eliminated or radically altered, and two thirds of the world's coral reefs have been degraded, 10 per cent of them "beyond recognition" (Lakshmi Narasaiah, 2005).

Causes of loss of biodiversity are generally grouped into two categories. The natural causes include floods, earthquakes, landslides, natural competition between species, lack of pollination and diseases. The most serious man-made threat to biological diversity are deliberate destruction of the ecosystem, especially the tropical rain forests, wetlands and coral reefs and disappearance of habitats, in the wake developmental activities like industrialisation, urbanisation, mining, construction of dams, deforestation, grazing, over-exploitation, fire etc. Truly speaking now there is no forest which could be named as virgin. In the process we are pushing the 'Earth' from the state of 'biodiversity rich' to' biodiversity deficit'.

The current decline in biological diversity is largely the result of human activity and major cause is population explosion. The Earth's resources are finite to meet peoples continued need. It is in the second half of the last century the impact of human population on environment and earth's finite resources could be felt as the ecological balance started losing. Excessive use coupled with lack of awareness about the actual and potential value of biological resources has led to the loss of biological diversity. Proof of this loss is the extinction of some wild species like Cheetah and some domesticated plant varieties and animal breeds.

The major proximate causes of species extinction are habitat loss and degradation affecting 89 per cent of all threatened birds, 83 per cent of mammals and 91 per cent of all threatened plants assessed globally (IUCN. 2000). The main causes of habitat loss are agricultural activities, extraction (including mining, fishing, logging and harvesting) and development (human settlements, industry and associated infrastructure). Habitat loss and fragmentation leads to the formation of isolated, small, scattered populations. These small populations are increasingly vulnerable to inbreeding depression, high infant mortality and susceptible to environmental stochasticity, and consequently, in the end, possible extinction. Changes in forest composition and quality, and the resultant habitat type lead to declines in primary food species for wildlife.

Exploitation such as hunting, collecting, fisheries and trade are a major threat to birds (37 per cent), mammals (34 per cent), plants (8 per cent of those assessed), reptiles and marine fishes. In India, poaching is another insidious threat that has emerged in recent years as one of the primary reasons for the decline in numbers of species, such as the tiger. Poaching pressures, however, are unevenly distributed since certain selected species are more heavily targeted than others are. Alien invasive species are a significant threat affecting 350 (30 per cent of all threatened) birds and 361 (15 per cent of all threatened) plant species. Islands are particularly susceptible to invasions of alien species.

Accelerated loss of biodiversity, largely on account of disempowerment of local communities, commercial exploitation, and fragmentation and degradation of habitats, has become cause of concern. The loss of biodiversity is being felt through greater water shortage and lack of fodder, fuel, other livelihood resources and so on. And with this there has been serious erosion in the knowledge base of people, especially the women and men of local communities, and of the cultural values linking people with nature.

The underlying causes of biodiversity loss, however, are poverty, macroeconomic policies, international trade factors, policy failures, poor environmental law/weak enforcement, unsustainable development projects and lack of local control over resources (Wood *et al.*, 2000).

Biodiversity Conservation and Sustainable Development

Sustainable development means development that meets the needs of the present without compromising the ability of future generations to meet their own needs. Thus 'Sustainable Development' becomes a goal not just for the developing nations, but for industrial ones as well. Sustainable development distributes the benefits of economic progress more equitably, protects both local and global environments for future generations and truly improves the quality of life (Khan and Shishodia, 2005).

It is useful and indeed necessary to remind ourselves that a healthy human environment depends entirely on biodiversity. Everything we eat, wear and produce on this planet Earth is ultimately dependent on its biodiversity, yet we behave as if it hardly matters. And while we ponder over the question of whether there is life on Mars, we seem to have forgotten that only a fraction of all species on Earth have been found and described, while countless others both known and still undiscovered are driven to extinction. We are now losing wild species at a rate that has been estimated to be 100 to 1000 times faster than the prehistoric background rate (Martin, 2002).

It seems equally ironic that whilst poverty reduction is rightly on everybody's mind, few recognise that the livelihood of the poorest 1.2 billion people on Earth depends either entirely or at least partly on wild resources. In this context the question may be raised as to whether measuring poverty based on a one or two dollar income is adequate, if the value of the goods and services provided by ecosystems is not included in the framework of national accounts. According to a World Bank study, for example, more than two billion people rely on traditional medicine. Thus, biodiversity conservation, and more specifically species conservation, must also be seen as an essential part of the maintenance of a healthy human environment and as crucial to the economic well-being of all societies. Threats that put species in danger are by this logic also a danger to humanity (Martin, 2002).

Agricultural Biodiversity

Agriculture now extends to cover about one third of the land surface, and is the largest user of biodiversity and its components. Projections suggest that global food production will need to double over the next half-century; either by intensification of existing production systems or by expansion into new lands. Either way, there will be major impacts on biodiversity. This means that the management of agricultural ecosystems has to be an essential part of any overall strategy for biodiversity conservation. Moreover, the productive management of agricultural biodiversity will be key to meeting future food needs while also maintaining or enhancing the other goods and services provided by agricultural ecosystems. For example :

- Better use of crop and livestock genetic resources will be key to achieving sustainable increases in food production, not only through breeding enhanced varieties and breeds, but also through a more intelligent deployment of genetic diversity in the field to reduce pest and disease outbreaks;

- Wider application of integrated pest management and of other approaches for the management of the components of biodiversity in agricultural ecosystems—such as pollinators, soil biota and the natural enemies of pests and diseases—can contribute to productivity increases and reduce the use of external inputs at the same time, learning, research, and adaptive management of agricultural biodiversity, in order to integrate ecosystem approaches into everyday management. After all, farmers comprise the largest group of ecosystem managers and there are important opportunities to engage them to improve the management of biodiversity in ecosystems (FAO, 2002).

Biodiversity conservation seeks to maintain life support systems provided by nature. The biodiversity' must be interpreted in a holistic sense, to encompass natural ecosystems, wild species and varieties, agricultural ecosystems and domesticated species and varieties, including related ecological and evolutionary processes. Conservationists believe in total protection and conservation of biodiversity whereas nations and people with commercial bent of mind advocate for protection of economically important species only. However, in a developed world biodiversity conservation and sustainable development must go side by side. This can achieved by sustainable use of biological resources, implying their use in such manner as will not imperil their long-term existence, or will not in other ways threaten biodiversity.

Constitutional Obligations and International Conventions

Article 48-A and Article 51-A (G) of the Directive Principles of State Policy in the Constitution of India state that 'the State shall endeavour to protect and improve the environment and to safeguard the forests and wildlife in the country", and 'to protect and improve the national environment including forests, lakes, rivers and wildlife, and to have compassion for the living creatures'.

Article-253 of the Indian constitution empowers the Parliament to make laws implementing India's International obligations, treaties and other forms of commitments. Several Acts like Water (Prevention and Control of Pollution) Act, 1974; Water (Prevention and Control of Pollution) Cess Act, 1977; Air Prevention and Control of Pollution Act, 1981; Environment (Protection) Act, 1986; Forest Conservation Act, 1980; Wildlife Protection Act, 1972; Biological Diversity Act, 2002 have been framed by the Parliament to confirm the view of the commitment of India for implementation of international treaties (Patnaik and Roy, 2006).

The concept of sustainable development emerged during United Nation's Conference on Human Environment popularly known as Stockholm Declaration of 1972. A focussed articulation of these concerns in programmes and policies was intensified after the Earth Summit held at Rio de Janeiro in 1992. One of the landmark results of the Earth Summit held in Rio de Janeiro in 1992 was the Convention on Biological Diversity (CBD) and India's becoming a party to the Convention on Biological Diversity (CBD). The Biodiversity Convention calls upon parties to conserve and sustainably use biological diversity while equitably sharing the benefits of the use of genetic resources and associated traditional knowledge (MoEF, 2001). These goals are key elements of sustainable development.

To date the Convention has been ratified by 178 countries and the European community, making it one of the most global of all international treaties. While other treaties deal with specific aspects of biodiversity, such as trade, particular ecosystems (wetlands or deserts, for example), geographic areas or species, the Convention on Biological Diversity has a broad, over-arching focus. Its scope is global, covering all components of biological diversity—from ecosystems and habitats, to species, genomes and genes. Other issues addressed include intellectual property rights, technology transfer, access to genetic resources, incentives, and the development of financial mechanisms to assist governments to implement the Convention (IUCN, 2002).

The CBD has proven not only to be at the heart of sustainable development but also to be capable of making the shift from policymaking to implementation. Biodiversity is humankind's biological life insurance. Implementation now is essential for the well-being of future generations and ourselves (Pronk, 2002).

Biodiversity and Agenda 21

- The broad vision for biodiversity in Agenda 21 of Rio Conference is its conservation and sustainable use accompanied by equitable benefit sharing mechanisms.
- his includes a focus on enhancing national biodiversity protection measures involving the development of national strategies; mainstreaming of biodiversity concerns; ensuring the fair and equitable sharing of the benefits accruing from biodiversity; country-wide studies on biodiversity; fostering traditional methods and indigenous knowledge, encouraging biotechnological innovations along with the equitable sharing of their benefits and promoting regional and international cooperation.
- It also called for reinforcing at the national and international level, capacities for the assessment, study, and systematic observation and evaluation of biodiversity.

CBD and NBSAP

- India is a signatory to the Convention on Biodiversity (CBD) and has been taking steps to conserve the unique and rich biodiversity of the country.
- With regard to biodiversity conservation, several steps like preparation of a National Action Plan, framing a legislation namely Biodiversity Conservation Act, 2002 followed by Biodiversity Conservation Rule, 2004; have been initiated to meet our commitments under the Convention.
- The NBSAP (National Biodiversity Strategy and Action Plan) envisages the assessment and stocktaking of biodiversity-related information at various levels.

- The international biodiversity strategy programme is also being organised by World Resource Institute, the World Conservation Union and United Nations Environment Programme (UNEP).

Traditional Biodiversity Related Knowledge (TBRK)

Traditional biodiversity related knowledge (TBRK) has the potential to play a key role in assisting global actions to ensure the sustainable use of biological resources. Indigenous TBRK is an existing knowledge base that can compliment scientific knowledge and provide decision-makers with more complete information on biological systems. More importantly, TBRK can provide a basis for indigenous communities to address issues of poverty' and food security in an increasingly global society.

Human societies have always relied on biological resources for physical and spiritual sustenance. Biodiversity ultimately provides us with a source of food, medicines, materials and opportunities. Indigenous peoples in common with all peoples have a right to derive a means of existence from the sustainable use of biological resources found within territorial borders according to cultural practices. This right is based on the long and close association between indigenous peoples and their traditional biological resources developed and in many cases maintained over thousands of years. This interdependence has created the diversity of cultures we see today and the diversity within biological systems commonly referred to as biodiversity. It is no small coincidence that the majority of the worlds remaining biodiversity reside in indigenous territories (Schnierer, 2002).

Intellectual Property Right, Biodiversity and Sustainable Development

IPRs (Intellectual Peoperty Rights) are an inherent compromise between private and public interests. They provide an incentive to private inventors to innovate, while at the same time seeking to ensure that the result of the innovation is disseminated. The TRIPS Agreement was the result of initiatives developed countries took in the 1970s and 1980s to address the growing trade impacts of counterfeit trademarks. The TRIPS Agreement was resisted by many developing countries, but as part of the multilateral trade agreements, it had to be accepted as part of the overall Uruguay Round package. As noted above, it sets forth a set of minimum standards for PRIs, which countries can expand upon (Tarasofsky, 2002).

Its inclusion in the Uruguay Round implies that along with all other WTO Agreements, the TRIPS Agreement must also support the objective of sustainable development and a high level of environmental protection (as expressed in the preamble to the Agreement Establishing the WTO). However, intellectual property rights raise a series of issues related to biodiversity conservation (Tarasofsky, 2002):

- Conventional (Western) intellectual property rights may not be adequate to fully protect he knowledge of indigenous and local people, who are often the custodians of biodiversity, thereby possibly depriving them of a potentially powerful incentive to conserve the biodiversity around them;
- Intellectual property rights can influence the negotiations of agreements on access to genetic resources, as well as the possibilities to share benefits equitably;
- Patent processes may not sufficiently safeguard against misappropriation of traditional and local knowledge;
- Implementation of intellectual property rights over improved plant varieties can lead to practices that displace traditional systems of informal innovation that may well have previously fostered agricultural biological diversity;
- Intellectual property rights might interfere with effective transfer of technology to developing countries.

The impact of intellectual property rights on the rights of local communities, consumers and the environment has become a major source of controversy. This is especially so after the TRIPS agreement in the WTO facilitated the worldwide patenting of life forms and biological materials, which has given rise to public concerns over the environment, food security, farmers' livelihoods and the rights of indigenous peoples over their knowledge and resources (Khor, 2002).

At the heart of the debate is the increasing misappropriation of traditional knowledge by corporations that are now patenting human genes, plants and other biological materials, many of which exist in nature or have been used for generations by farmers and indigenous peoples (Khor, 2002).

Plant genetic resources represent arguably the most important category of all biological resources because of their importance in food production. The global seed market for modern crop varieties is estimated at US$30 billion a year. But this figure does not include the wild and semi-domesticated relatives of modern crops nor so called 'landraces' (folk varieties), all of which also have considerable economic value as well as social, cultural and spiritual importance that cannot be quantified in monetary terms.

Most of the states that are relatively rich in biodiversity are developing countries located in the tropics, but while these countries may be in a relatively strong position to benefit from trade in their genetic resources for pharmaceutical development, their bargaining position with the seed industry is weak. A new plant-based drug tends to be derived from a single natural compound, usually by a company in the North using material from the South. A new crop variety, by contrast, often results from generations of selection and breeding, frequently in many different parts of the world, making a fair division of benefits well-nigh impossible. Supply and demand is also much less clear-cut when it comes to suitable crop germplasm. Countries are much more interdependent, and ultimately all countries are dependent upon exotic genetic materials (Middleton, 2004).

However, although research and development of new plant breeds is based mainly on modern, well-understood varieties, wild species or landraces are still crucial to future innovations. When collections of modern varieties fail to provide effective protection against a pest or disease, researchers have to turn to 'new' genes that are undiscovered by scientists or known only to indigenous or traditional communities. For this reason among many others, the conservation of the planet's biodiversity remains important to us all, and despite the considerable difficulties involved in apportioning property rights to genetic resources, there is a pressing need to resolve these issues (Middleton, 2004).

Biopiracy

Unscrupulous investors have been trying to patent genetic varieties, often when it is clear that they have not "invented" anything, but are simply taking advantage of traditional knowledge. For example, in 1994 the president of the U.S. seed company POD-NERS bought yellow beans in Sonora, Mexico. He brought them home, bred several generations, selecting for yellow seeds. In 1996 the company had produced a "uniform and stable variety with yellow seeds", and applied for a patent. In 1999 a U.S. patent (and Plant Variety Protection Certificate) was granted. In 1999 the company was suing Mexican bean exporters for patent infringement (Bryant, 2005).

Biodiversity Conservation

Biodiversity loss—pose a serious threat to development. 'Ecologically destructive economic activities are inefficient not merely because of the resulting resource misallocation but also because of the (excessive) scale of activity levels; excessive in relation to the limited availability of natural capital when the latter is complementary to human-made capital' (Foy and Daly, 1989). In order to bring about sustainable resource conservation and management, it is essential to adopt several different approaches for managing our forests and biodiversity.

There is also the need for greater involvement of communities, and for models which decentralise of management and conservation roles and responsibilities. As of now, there are still major lacunae in information resources pertaining to forests, biodiversity-flora and fauna, causative factors for their degradation, and major threats. The available data is alarmingly inadequate to provide a lucid picture of the current status and ongoing losses/gains. More importantly, laws and policies governing natural resources are still not sufficient enough to tackle the scale of the problem, and these insufficiencies have not been addressed with a sense of urgency.

In this section, we provide some indicators of the biological policy, technological, and institutional issues that will help mitigate the disturbingly accelerating biodiversity loss.

Conservation Strategies

Expansion of the Protected Area Network : Maintaining viable populations of species, whether plant or animal, is a crucial factor in biodiversity conservation and this requires the appropriate conservation of important ecosystems and habitats. Currently, the country has 88 national parks, and 490 sanctuaries. In 1988, Rodgers and Panwar suggested that the percentage of the country's area under the protected area network, which was then only 3.3 per cent, be enhanced to 4.6 per cent. The recent update of the Rodgers and Panwar report (Rodgers, Panwar and Mathu, 2000) suggests that the area under parks and sanctuaries be increased to 160 National Parks and 698 sanctuaries accounting for 5.69 per cent of the country's geographical total.

Population Surveys and Assessments and Database Creation: To design a proper strategy for conservation, adequate data on species diversity, populations, location and extent of habitat, major threats to different species, etc. and changes in these aspects overtime are not available. Given our extensive diversity, ecological surveys and taxonomic investigations need to be intensified, particularly for plants and insects. For conducting ecological studies, species for such studies can be prioritised including keystone species, large mammals, migratory species, etc. The country's wildlife institutions need to network and coordinate their activities so that priority issues and areas are identified.

Mapping of Forest Types, Protected Areas, and Natural Forests: It is important to generate maps of the protected areas of the country showing their contiguity with the existing reserve and protected forests. This will provide a way for determining possible corridors, habitat contiguity, and buffer zones and facilitate biodiversity conservation. Further, vegetation mapping according to forest types needs to be done for the entire country.

Improved Protection Efforts and a Landscape Approach to Conservation : Owing to habitat fragmentation and consequent losses suffered by different populations, there is need for ensuring the safety of the biodiversity lying outside our protected areas. Population viability analyses for different species have revealed that the loss of even a single individual from a small isolated population could adversely affect the population structure and viability and push many species towards extinction. The need of the hour is a landscape approach to conservation where protected and non-protected areas are integrated through significant protection measures initiated at both the state and local community levels (Gadgil *et al.*, 1996)

In Situ Conservation : In situ conservation, the conservation of species in their natural habitats, is the most appropriate way of conserving biodiversity. Conserving the areas where populations of species exist naturally is a underlying condition for the conservation of biodiversity. That's why protected areas form a central element of any national strategy to conserve biodiversity. A protected area is a geographically defined area that is designated or regulated and managed to achieve specific conservation objectives. This includes national parks and nature reserves, sustainable use reserves, wilderness areas and heritage sites.

The Convention on Biological Diversity recognises *in situ* conservation as the primary approach for biodiversity conservation. Article 8 of the Convention provides the main set of Convention obligations to conserve biological diversity.

Ex Situ Conservation and Species Reintroduction : Captive breeding aims at maintaining viable and healthy genetic captive stocks in conservation facilities and is meant to supplement *in situ* initiatives. Captive breeding can provide animals for possible reintroduction to the wild at a later stage or for supplementing current populations with new stock. *In situ* measures, however, are always preferred, since in most cases it is cheaper to protect populations in their natural habitat than to reintroduce captive-bred ones.

Because of limitations of space, finances, and facilities in the institutions that undertake captive breeding, species prioritisation is a primary concern. An overwhelming 91 per cent of animals kept in Indian zoos are non-threatened, yet take up much of the space and resources of zoos (Walker, 2000). Zoos in India may need to restrict their efforts to a few species that can benefit from captive breeding initiatives, such as small-bodied species of Chiroptera, Rodentia, and Insectivora. These make up 60 per cent of mammalian taxa in the country and are easier to reintroduce than larger mammals (Walker, 2000).

Combating the Wildlife Trade : The international wildlife trade, worth billions of dollars annually, has caused massive declines in the numbers of many species of animals and plants. The scale of over-exploitation for trade aroused such concern for the survival of species that an international treaty was drawn up in 1973 to protect wildlife, against such over-exploitation and to prevent international trade from threatening species with extinction.

Known as CITES, the Convention on International Trade in Endangered Species of Wild Fauna and Flora, entered into force on 1 July 1975 and now has a membership of 146 countries. These countries act by banning commercial international trade in an agreed list of endangered species and by regulating and monitoring trade in others that might become endangered.

Information Networking : In the absence of a system/ mechanism (state-sponsored or otherwise), for effective sourcing and pooling of information, there is often colossal wastage of money and efforts in recreating such data. Promoting networking and sharing of information through government-controlled and private agencies is essential for an informed and inexpensive approach to biodiversity conservation.

Geographical Information Systems and Remote Sensing in Planning and Monitoring : Utilisation of G1S (Geographical Information Systems) and remote sensing could help determine the rates, causes, and scale of biodiversity loss. Information on deforestation and land-use change can be integrated with data on the distribution of biodiversity and existing information on soils, topography, climate, etc. to obtain a comprehensive picture. GIS must be used more extensively as a tool in policy and landscape level planning.

Creation of New Conservation Reserves : New types of legally recognised reserves should be created where sustainable utilisation and community involvement will be the norm. Currently only national parks and sanctuaries are legal entities, which were created largely on the exclusionary principle.

Protection of Traditional Knowledge : Parties to the WTO and CBD, in cooperation with civil society, should:

- provide assistance and training for holders of traditional knowledge in the negotiation, drafting, implementation, and enforcement of contracts involving use of their knowledge, as well as evaluating the impacts of those contracts on the protection of traditional knowledge;
- apply Article 30 of the TRIPS Agreement (exceptions to rights conferred) to ensure that patent information can be used by third parties for research into technologies relevant to biodiversity conservation;
- exclude from patentability existing traditional/indigenous knowledge and essentially derived products and processes from such knowledge, unless the affected community explicitly consents;
- establish traditional knowledge databases or registers to prevent piracy of this knowledge (Tarasofsky, 2002).

Community-oriented Approaches : An important factor contributing to the endangered status of many species is anthropogenic activity. Populations dependent on local forests also contribute to species endangerment by over-exploiting forest produce in the absence of livelihood alternatives. There is need for involving people and their knowledge base for protection and management of biodiversity. Therefore, local communities who influence conservation, management, and utilisation of biodiversity are major stakeholders in its conservation.

- *Eco-tourism and Recreation Forestry :* In order to conserve forests and to offer incentives to local communities and private parties, eco-tourism and recreation forestry activities such as wildlife watching, adventure tourism, nature trails, hiking, camping, angling, arid water sports can be considered. This will provide monetary returns to the forest department, while ensuring that biodiverse patches are protected with support of the local community.

- *Biodiversity Registers :* One of the clauses in the Convention on Biological Diversity lays down that where utilisation of the knowledge, innovations and practices of local and indigenous communities leads to benefits, such benefits should be equitably shared with the holders of such knowledge, innovation and practices.

  Documentation of this knowledge becomes important, as this will not only serve as evidence for the rightful claim of the originator community for benefits arising out of that knowledge, but also prevent the knowledge from getting lost over time. One method of that is being used to document the knowledge and skills of local communities related to biological resources is through Community Biodiversity Registers. The resister process seeks to document the knowledge of conservation, as well as economic uses of biodiversity resources that rest with India's local communities (Gadgil *et al.,* 1996).

BIOPROSPECTING INVOLVING LOCAL COMMUNITIES

The Kani Tribals and Tropical Botanic Garden and Research Institute (TBGRI)

The TBGRI, Thiruvanthapuram, Kerala developed a drug Jeevani from *Trichopus zeylanicus,* a plant whose fruits were traditionally eaten by the Kani tribals to provide energy and agility. A licence to manufacture this drug was given to Arya Vaidya Pharmacy (Coimbatore) Limited for a period of 7 years for Rs 1 million of which the tribals were to receive 50 per cent of the licence fee as well as 50 per cent of the royalty obtained by TBGRI on the sale of the drug. In December 1987, this plant was discovered when scientists of TBGRI on a bioprospecting trip to the Western Ghats, noticed that their tribal guides gained energy after eating the fruits of this plant. The leaves of this plant with some other ingredients was later developed into Jeevani. This agreement received criticism for its inequitable nature because of the lack of involvement of the entire Kani community, and failure to take permission from the Kani medical practitioners who are the guardians of this knowledge (Anuradha, 2000).

Reviving Agricultural Traditions—A Success Story

After the Green Revolution of the 1960s in India, farmers in the hilly regions of Tehri Garwal district of Uttaranchal started using high input-intensive techniques for farming to increase productivity. New "improved' seeds of high yielding varieties were introduced here, along a range of pesticides, fertilisers and other external inputs. In the race for modernisation, the farmers began to rapidly lose their traditional systems of sustainable agriculture. This was the basis of the 'Save the Seeds Movement' or 'Beej Bachao Andolan' (BBA) (Suryanarayanan *et al.,* 1999).

A group of villagers, led by farmer and social activist Vijay Jardari from Jardhargaon, stated visiting remote villages in search of varieties of traditional seeds. The group collected as many as 250 varieties of rice, 170 of kidney beans and many others, which had been presumed, lost in the region. In the course of this search, a wealth of information was documented for the first time. During their search BBA activists found that in the valley of Ramasirain farmers, grew a distinctive variety of red rice called *chardhan* (four grains). The rice was nutritious and did not require huge external inputs. Another remarkable traditional system of cropping which came to light was *barnaja,* where twelve crops are simultaneously frown in the same field. This not only avoided monoculture, but also helped restore soil fertility and ensure food security.

Conclusion

Indian civilisation is ancient and presently it is among highest population densities in the world. It still retains much of its rich heritage of biodiversity. This diversity is life support system upon which families, communities, nations and future generations depend. The future of country's economic well-being lies closely interlinked with conservation of our biological resources. Sustainable use of biological resources holds key to biodiversity conservation. There is also the need for greater involvement of communities, and for models which decentralise of management and conservation roles and responsibilities. In the beginning of 21st Century, in an era globalisation, privatisation and liberalisation, our rich biological resource base and traditional biodiversity related knowledge (TBRK) is threatened due to partisan WTO sanctions such as laws relating to IPRs and patent acts. The broad vision for conservation of biodiversity Agenda 21 of Rio Conference for a sustainable society need to be translated into reality through awareness of common man to intelligentsia about the actual and potential value of biological resources and its sustainable use.

References

Anuradha R V. (2000) Sharing the Benefits of Biodiversity: the Kani-TBGRI Deal in Kerala, India. Community-based Conservation in South Asia: Case Study 1 Pune: *Kalpavriksh and International Institute of Environment and Development.* 43 pp.

Bryant. Peter J. (2005) Value of Biodiversity. In : *BIODIVERSITY and CONSERVATION*—A Hypertext Book. School of Biological Sciences, University of California, Irvine, CA 92697, USA. *http://datwin.bio.uci.edu/*~sustain/bio65/ lec11/ b651ec11.htm.

FAO (2002) An Ecosystem Approach for Agriculture. Interdepartmental Working Group on Biodiversity, Food and Agriculture Organisation). *Biodiversity and Sustainable Development, CBD News Supplement,* Secretariat of the Convention on Biological Diversity, 393 Saint-Jacques St., Suite 300, Montreal, Quebec, H2Y 1N9 Canada, p.5

Foy, G and Daly, H. (1989) Allocation, Distribution and Scale as Determinants of Environmental Degradation: Case Studies of Haiti, El Salvador and Costa Rica, Washington D C: *World Bank.*

Gadgil, M; Singh, S. N.; Nagendra, H. and Chandran, M. D. S. (1996) In Situ Conservation of Wild Relatives of Cultivated Plants: Guiding Principles and a Case Study. Bangalore: *FAO, Rome and Indian Institute of Science.* 21 pp. *http://www.biodiv.org/doc/world/in/in-nr-02-en.pdf.*

Gadgil, Madhav *et al.* (1996) Peoples Biodiversity Registers, *Amruth,* Vol. 1. Issue 5, October 1996.

Gadgil, Madhav (2005) Diversity –The Cornerstone of Life. *Vigyan Prasar, New Delhi and Sanctuary Magazine, Mumbai.* 64 pp.

IUCN (2002) Biodiversity is Life. *Gland, Switzerland: The World Conservation Union*

IUCN. (2000) Red List of Threatened Species. *Gland, Switzerland: The World Conservation Union.*

Khan, T.I. and Shioshodia, Y.S. (2005) *Biodiversity Conservation and Sustainable Development.* Second Revised and Enlarged Edition. Jaipur, 410 p.

Khor, Martin (2002) *Intellectual Property, Biodiversity and Sustainable Development: Resolving the Difficult Issues.* Zed Books, Third World Network, p. 104.

Lakshmi Narasaiah, M. (2005) *Biodiversity and Sustainable Development.* New Delhi, Discovery, 176 p.

Martin, Claude (2002) Meeting Sustainable Development Goals Without Endangering Species Diversity. *Biodiversity and Sustainable Development, CBD News Supplement,* Secretariat of the Convention on Biological Diversity, 393 Saint-Jacques St., Suite 300, Montreal, Quebec, H2Y 1N9 Canada, p. 7.

Middleton, Nick (2004) *Biodiversity, Trade and Intellectual Property Rights: Seeds and Plants. Convention on Biological Diversity (CBD).* Middleton Publication Biodiversity, pdf.

MoEF. (1999) *National Policy and Macrolevel Action Strategy on Biodiversity.* New "Delhi: Ministry of Environment and Forests, Government of India, p. 74.

MoEF. (2001) India's Second National Report to the Convention on Biological Diversity. *New Delhi: Ministry of Environment and Forests, Government of India.*

Myers, N.; Mittermeier, R. A.; Mittermeier, C. G.; da Fonseca, GAB and Kents, J. (2000) Biodiversity Hotspots for Conservation Priorities. *Nature,* 403: 853-858.

Olson, D. M. and Dinerstein, E. (1998) *The Global 200: A Representation Approach to Conserving the Earth's Distinctive Ecoregions USA:* World Wildlife Fund.

Patnaik, B.K. and Roy, D. (2006) India's International Obligations and Legal Framework for Environmental Management and Biodiversity Conservation. National Conference on *"Biodiversity Conservation for a Sustainable Society",* Nayagarh College, Nayagarh, Orissa, Aug. 26-27, 2006. Abstract, p. 67.

Pronk, Jan (2002) Biodiversity is Humankind's Life Insurance. *Biodiversity and Sustainable Development. CBD News Supplement,* Secretariat of the Convention on Biological Diversity,

393 Saint-Jacques St., Suite 300, Montreal, Quebec, H2Y 1N9 Canada, p. 5.

Rodgers, W.A.; Panwar, H. S. and Mathur, V. B. (2000) *Wildlife Protected Area Network in India: A Review (Executive Summary).* Dehra Dun : Wildlife Institute of India. 44 pp.

Schnierer, Stephan (2002) Traditional Knowledge and Sustainable Development. *Biodiversity and Sustainable Development, CBD News Supplement,* Secretariat of the Convention on Biological Diversity, 393 Saint-Jacques St., Suite 300, Montreal, Quebec, H2Y 1N9 Canada, p. 14-15.

Suryanarayanan, J. *el al.,* (1999) Regeneraing Forests, Traditional Irrigation and Agro-biodiversity : Community Based Conservation in Jardhargaon, Uttar Pradesh, India, Kalpavriksh.

Tarasofsky, R.G. (2002). *Towards a Mutually Supportive Relationship Between the Convention on Biological Diversity and the World Trade Organisation: An Action Guide.* IUCN, Gland, Switzerland and Cambridge, UK. v + 26pp.

Walker, S. (2000) CBSG Regional Networks as Conservation Engineers: India as a Case Study. In : *International Zoo Yearbook,* 37:1-17. The Zoological Society of London, London.

Wood, A.; Stedman-Edwards, P. and Mang, J. (2000) *The Root Causes of Biodiversity Loss.* UK: *World Wide Fund for Nature. Earthscan Publications.* 399 pp.

2

CONSERVATION OF BIODIVERSITY, PROSPECTS AND CONCERN

*Prof. S.P. Rath**

"Biological diversity" term was first of all put forward by Norse and McManus (1980). It contains two concepts *i.e.* genetic diversity and ecological diversity. The term again shortened as "Biodiversity" by W.G.Rosen in 1985. Biodiversity includes all life forms, ecosystems and ecological processes. However, the credit for popularity of this word goes to E.O Wilson, who is often called as the "Father of Biodiversity". Biodiversity is defined as 'the variability among living organisms from all sources, including terrestrial, marine and other aquatic ecosystems and the ecological complexes of which they are apart; this includes diversity within species, between species and,of ecosystems'. It is the manifestations of all types of diversity which are found at all the levels of organism. It includes entire range of varieties not only species but also all subunits of species like subspecies, race, and variety among the living organism important to global environment. Man himself an important integral part of the global biodiversity.

Levels of biodiversity

1. Genetic Diversity: It is the variation of genes within the species. It brings distinction among the individuals within a population or varieties within one species. It is due to variation in the genes and also the influence of environment. Loss of genetic diversity leads to genetic erosion.

2. Species Diversity: It refers to the variety of species in particular region Species diversity depends on genetic diversity as well as environmental condition. Hence, Tundra supports less species diversity while species diversity is peak in tropical region.

* Head of the Botany Department, Aska Science College, Aska.

3. Ecological Diversity: This represents the number of species in a community. It deals with the difference between ecosystem types, including the habitat diversity and ecological processes in an ecosystem type. Patterns of energy flow and water cycle are distinct in each ecosystem.

Types of Diversity: (Diversity Indices)

1. Alpha (α) Diversity: Species diversity within a community or habitat, comprises two components *i.e.* species richness and evenness. Sometimes dominance of one Vegetation stratum may effect the a diversity of the other strata.

2. Beta (β) Diversity: It is the inter-community diversity expressing the rate of species turnover per unit change in habitat.

3. Gamma (γ) Diversity: It is the overall diversity at landscape level includes both α and β diversities.

$$\gamma = \alpha + \beta + Q$$

Q - Total number of habitats or communities

α - Average value of diversities

β - Average value of β diversities

The earth is believed to be nearly 5 billion years old. Life began nearly 3 to 4 billion years ago and the first plant came to exist for more then 3 billion years back. It has been predicted that man involved on earth about 3 to 4 million years back. From this geological time scale, it is found that a self-sustaining ecosystem was made about a half billion years ago. Due to interaction between different trophic level and with their environment, an ever-extending diversity has been created. This interaction only increases the number and variety of species. All the species do not exist alone. There are interactions, within themselves which form the foundation to their proper functioning.

The total number of plant and animal species may range from 5 to 30 million that may exist on earth. Out of that 1.5 million species of animal, nearly 250000 species of vascular plants and about 800000 species of lower plants are identified.

Biodiversity increase from poles to the equator and from high attitudes to low attitudes. Terrestrial communities normally have greater diversity per unit area. The stable and colder climate supports high speciation rates due to more sedentary population and hence, geographical isolation and more opportunities for selection. Therefore, diversity on the earth is uneven. Plants that provide 90 per cent of the world's foods were developed from ancient wild plants growing mainly in the tropics. A large number of species have been exploited to serve as food and other basic needs. These wild plants and animal species may have a role in curing dreadful diseases also.

The estimated numbers of species globally are as below:

Flora Group	*No. of species*	*Animal*	*Species*
Bacteria	4000	Mammals	4321
Bga	1700	Birds	12450
Algae	40000	Reptiles	6300
Fungi	72,000	Amphibians	4184
Bryophytes	17,000	Fishes	23,000
Gymnosperms	750	Insects	1025000
Angiosperms	2.5 lakhs	Molluscs	7000
		Protozoans	110000

There are 12 megadiversity centers in the world and India is one of them. India has 10 biogeographical zones and 25 biotic provinces. India has 5 world heritage sites, 12 biosphere reserves and 6 Ramsar Wetlands. Among the 25 hotspots in the world, two are found in India. 1. Eastern Himalaya, 2. Western Ghats. India is a homeland of 49219 plant species of which 5150 are endemic and distributed into 141 genera under 47 families it covers nearly 7 per cent of the flora. The 10 biogeographical regions are: 1. Trans Himalaya, 2. Himalaya, 3. Desert, 4. semi-arid, 5. Western Ghats, 6. Deccan Peninsula, 7. Gangetic plain, 8. North East, 9. Coasts, 10. Islands.

The number of species of flora and fauna in India:

Flora

Taxon	*Number of species*
Bacteria	850
Algae	6500
Fungi	14,500
Lichen	2000
Bryophyte	2850
Pteridophyta	11000
Gymnosperms	64
Angiosperms	17500

Animal species

Group	*Number of species*
Mammals	300
Birds	1232
Reptiles	456
Amphibians	209
Fishes	2546
Insects	60,000
Molluscs	5070
Protozoal	2577

As many as 167 species of crops 320 species of wild crop relatives and several species of domesticated animals have originated in India. Following examples are showing their number of varieties:

Rice	50000 varieties	Cattle	27 breeds
Mango	10000 varieties	Goats	22 breeds
Sorghum	5000 varieties	Sheep	40 breeds
Pepper	500 varieties	Poultry	18 breeds
		Buffalo	8 breeds

India is considered to be center of origin of 30000 to 50000 varieties of rice, pigeon pea, mango, turmeric, ginger, sugarcane, gooseberries etc. Ranks 7th in terms of contribution of world agriculture.

Biodiversity in the State of Orissa

Orissa is a small state and geologically it is a part of Gondwana land mass one of the oldest and most stable land masses in the world. The state is gifted with perennial water resources with the presence of big rivers.,Asia's largest salt water lake Chilika and the unique mangrove swamp Bhitarkanika are on the coast. In its mountains and hills Orissa has Similipal-Meghasan (1,162 meters), Malayagiri (1,110 meters), Mankadnacha (1,110 meters), Mahendragiri (1,525 meters), Sinagaraz (1,516 meters), Devagiri (1,363 meters). One of the highest peaks of Eastern Ghats—Deomali (1,670 meters) has enhanced the geographical prominence of the state. The state is endowed with rich forest wealth. Once upon a time the forest cover in the state was said to be nearly 40 per cent of its total land area. But now it is reduced to about a mere 13 per cent only.

Chilika Lagoon(Wetland Heritage)

Chilika, the largest brackish water lake or lagoon of Asia. The lagoon's contribution in the field of floral species is significant. The lagoon is endowed with 352 angiospermic species. The lake hosts over 150 species of birds out of which 32 per cent aquatic, 22 per cent waders and about 46 per cent are terrestrial birds. Apart from all that lake abounds with various fish species like mullest, cat fishes, clupeoids, perches, threadfins, and sciaenids, prawns, crabs etc.

Justful Exploitation and proper management of resources can only save Chilika lake for posterity. The lake is to be prevented from being silted. The Nature and Wildlife Society of Orissa, the Orissa Environmental Society, the Bombay Natural History Society and United Artists association are conducting survey mass mobilisation campaign for protection of this Wetland Heritage.

Similipal Forest Heritage

It is a unique habitat of mixed tropical forest heritage in the Eastern Ghat. It is just 60 kilometers from Baripada. It supports a number of flora and fauna which are categorised as endangered, vulnerable, threatened and rare. It has many medicinal plants and nearly 92 orchids species. The faunal species like elephant, tiger, panther, wild boar, gaur, Asiatic wolf and four horned are found. It also supports about 233 species birds.

Gradual depletion of the forest is a great hindrance on the part of Similpal in reserving naturalness. A tiger project was established in 1973 and it was declared as a wild life sanctuary in 1979.

Mahendragiri(the epitome of genetic diversity)

It is one of the oldest forest ecosystem situated in Gajapati district on Eastern Ghat. It is the richest one so far as the genetic diversity is concerned. The vegetation can be classified into four types: 1. Sal forests; 2. Mixed forests; 3. Grasslands and 4. Shrubs. There are more than 650 species of flowering plants and many types of fern are found. Many of them are listed as rare in endangered in the IUCN East. There are 36 orchid species which are listed as rare and endemic. It supports fauna like leopard, elephant, boar, spored deer, tiger, hyena, wolves, musk rat, python, garden lizard, and nearly 20 types of snakes.

Due to shifting cultivation the wild life is depleting fast. Sri. Gopinath Gagapti Narayan Dave pleaded of conservation of Mahendragiri and it must be protected as a biosphere reserve.

Vhitarkanika (Orissa's mangroves)

Vhitarkanika mangrove swamp ecosystem is located in Kendrapada Dirstrict. It supports mainly mangrove plants like Avicennia officinalis, xylocarpus molucornsis, rhizophora mucronata, Aegiceras corniculation etc. it is also gifted with many aquatic fauna like salt water crocodile and many rare reptiles (olive ridley) in the jungle animals like wild boar, chital, jackal, hyena, porcupine, mongoose, python and king cobra are found. Birds like white ibies, pelicans, open billed storks, brahminy duck are also seem.

An immediate protection and conservation of Vhitarkanika is much warranted.

Importance of Biological Diversity

Biological diversity is the foundation upon which human civilisations are built. Development of early societies was supported by thousands of species of plants and animals. Man evolved from hunting and gathering substances to agricultural and industrial level of organisation. Biodiversity is important by the following ways:

1. Most of our food requirement is being met by various plants and living organisms. To fulfill the food demand of future generation, we have to rely on better strains of plants from the wild source. There are over 3000 species of food plants, of which only 150 species are source of food. Two-third of food is being produced by 3 carbohydrates rich crops—wheat, maize and rice;
2. Major plants like soyabean, coconut, peanut, sunflower, safflower, rapeseed, mustard and oilpalm are the source of fats and oil;
3. Resources required for medicine and industry are also very high. Most of the plants have medicinal value. One out of every 125 species has produced a major drug. They contain chemicals, which have specific effects on human body. These chemicals include alkaloids, resin, essential oil, fatty acid, latex etc. Unfortunately, very few plant species have been screened and many plants may even become extinct before their investigations. Only 1100 of worlds 365000 known species of plant have so far been examined for their medicinal properties. In India 3000 plants have been mentioned in books of which only 200 are used in bulk;
4. All the life forms are more significant in light of the emergent field of genetic engineering. If this new technology wants to fulfil its promise, then it needs as much genetic variability as possible;
5. For improvement of crop plants, plant breeders quite often depend on the genetic variability contained in the old indigenous verities of crops or their wild relatives. By this genetic variability it can possible to introduce much desired qualities of disease resistance and hardness in the cultivated plants;
6. Diversities of species and animals, birds etc. add new dimension to the beauty of the nature. Life becomes

enjoyable due to varieties of wildlife, as they are a source of recreation;

7. In water catchments and riparian areas vegetation act as a buffer and helps in maintaining movement and storage of water within biosphere (atmosphere, lithosphere and hydrosphere) and regulates run off (water that moves on the land especially along a slope, instead of entering into soil);
8. Vegetation stabilises the climates in the local areas and has a cooling effect on the environment;
9. It protects ecosystem integrity by regulating nutrient, mineral cycling;
10. Plants protect soil by binding the soil particles and also enhance soil fertility by adding organic matter;
11. Historically people have linked with certain plants and animals like Tulsi, Pipal, Khejri etc. they are planted and worshipped. Many birds, snakes and wild animals are worshipped. Every country and states takes pride in recognising a plant or animal as symbol of national or cultural heritage.

Causes of Loss of Biodiversity

Loss of biological diversity proceeds in small increments. Gradually it assumes dangerous proportions. Species once lost can't be replace. Loss of one species threatens others. Hence survival of man may also be under threat with the loss of biodiversity.

Following are the causes of loss of biodiversity:

1. Over population, large number of cattle herds, growing demand for land, energy and water supply. Nearly 20 per cent of the world population is living in the terrestrial biodiversity hotspots. Expanding human population has increased the exploitation of resources and altered land use pattern. This has resulted in fragmentation of habitats, ecosystem and landscape;
2. Unplanned developmental works and over exploitation of resources. Over exploitation has not only resulted in scarcity of materials but also left our biodiversity

exposed to various ecological threats and even extinction;

3. Forest has been reduced to 55 per cent of its original cover. Nearly 40 per cent of all species occur in the tropical forests. The topical forests are being destroyed systematically leading to the loss of several species of plants and animals from the natural habitats;
4. The growing human population generates different type of pollutants, which are being introduced to the ecosystem. Many of these pollutants directly or indirectly affect the survival of sensitive plants and animals in their natural habitats and thus lead to their extinction;
5. Destruction of habitats also leads to the extinction of a large numbers of species of plants and animals. This destruction may be due to conversion of forests to cropland by shifting cultivation for establishments of industries or human settlements as well as construction of dams;
6. Due to production of high yield varieties of hybrid plants, the plants with original genetic verities are eliminated, as they are not economically superior to the hybrid strains. Revolution in different field like green revolution for production of new varieties of plants with high yield, Blue revolution in fish production, white revolution in milk production, and afforestation with high yielding monocultures has posed one of the greatest threats to the world's genetic diversity in livestock, fish, crop and trees. The seeds used in the green revolution was hungry in terms of chemical fertilisers. The land of some states are diseased and dead due to huge application of chemical fertilisers and pesticides. People has to bear the cost of polluted food or poisoned food. As a result of green revolution we are self sufficient in food but we are all physically affected due to intake of poisoned food. Utilisation of chemical fertiliser, pesticides, insecticides and herbicides for increasing yielding capacity is also one cause;

7. Non-native species are introduce for their economic and other uses. They often become invasive and drive away the local species, these species are considered to be second major cause of extinction. Exotic species like *Eichhornia crassipers* was introduced in India to reduce pollution but it has clogged water bodies and result in death of aquatic plants and animals. Similarly 1859 an Australian farmer imported one dozen pair of rabbits for game. In six years population was 22 million. In 1930 it was 750 millions causing destruction of all types of vegetation;
8. 77 tree species are already extinct (WWF) and 976 tree species are critically endangered and facing extinction. About 80 per cent of the world's 100000 tree species are in tropics. Largest numbers of critically endangered species are found in Malaysia.

Looking at the grave situation of world biodiversity, IUCN (International Union for Conservation of Nature and Natural Resource) now know as the world Conservation Union prepared of species showing various categories of extinction risk in 1988. These documents are known as *Red Data Book or Red Data List.*

The loss of valuable plants is a matter of great concern. Man has become concerned about the importance of the conservation of biodiversity for the benefit of human race following the Stockholm conference, declaration of 1972 and the outcome of the UN charter for Nature of 1982 and the biodiversity convention in the Earth Summit of 1992.

It is seldom realised that the world's first recorded conservation measures were enacted in India during the 3rd century B.C. Emperor Ashoka had set up hospitals and reserves for wild animals and birds. Nearly 925 animals and 1014 plants are facing high risk of extinction. The number of critically endangered animals and plants in India is 18 and 44 respectively.

Example: Sus salvanius, Berberis nilghiriensis. In India the number of animals and plants are found to be endangered are 54 and 113 respectively.

Some Endangered Species of India

Vol.1 of the 'Red Data Book of Indian plants covering 235 endangered and rare species. Vol. 2 of the Red Data Book of Indian plants containing about 200 rare and endangered is completed. According to Red Data Book and lUCN's report, the extinction rate in India is the highest in the world . Western Ghat is experiencing some *Kilodeath*. *Kilodeath* means a situation of extinction rate of species are a thousand times higher than the normal.

Some Endangered Plant Species of India

1. Abies-delavayi
2. Taxus baccata
3. Picea brachytyla
4. Psilotum nudum
5. Angiopteris erecta
6. Adiandra griffithi
7. Vanilla pilifere
8. Rauvolfia serpentina
9. Atropa acuminata
10. Coptis teeta
11. Saussura bracteata
12. Strychnos nux-vomica
13. Nepenthes khasiana
14. Abutilon ranadeii
15. Delphinum malbaricum
16. Dipteris wallichii
17. Acrostichem aureum
18. Ophioglossum gramineum
19. Marsilea quadrifoli

Some Endangered Animal Species of India

1. Python reticulates
2. Python molures

3. Varanus salvator
4. Ertmochelys imbricata
5. Catreus wallichii
6. Lophophorus impejanus
7. Tragopn melanocephallus
8. Syphotides indica
9. Buceros bicornis
10. Ardeotis nigrices
11. Cursories bitoquates
12. Hemitragus hylocrius
13. Trigylus memmina
14. Cervus elephes hangle
15. Tetraceres quadricornis
16. Bubalus bubalus
17. Asinus heminus khur
18. Rhinoceros unicornis
19. Elephas indicus
20. Ailuresfulgens
21. Melures ursimus
22. Ursus arctos isabellinus
23. Canis alpinus
24. Canis lupus
25. Felis viverrina
26. Panthera uncia
27. Neofelis nebulosa
28. Hylobats hoolock
29. Presbyts johni
30. Moschus moschiferus

Conservation of Biodiversity

Conservation is defined as sound preservation, management and rational use of the available renewable natural resources. So conservation of biodiversity is defined as "safeguarding the varieties of complex biological communities or species of the earth, which have roles for the environment". This was the major issue at the 1992 Earth summit in Rio de Janerio (Brazil) well known as the convention on biological diversity signed by 153 countries. So all countries have a right to use it to improve the quality of life, but they are also responsible for conserving their biological diversity by using it in a controlled way. Biodiversity can be conserved by the following ways:

Ex Situ Conservation: In this practice plants and animals to be protected are removed from their natural habited and are placed in a safer area under the control of man. Such as botanical garden, zoo, seed bank, gene bank, germplasm bank etc.

In Situ Conservation: It means on-site conservation that is protection of species at their natural habitats. It includes wild life sanctuaries, national park and biosphere reserves:

1. Sustainable use—means the level of exploitation, or use of resources should not exceed the ability of ecosystem to replace or regenerate itself. Our logging practices should be equitable to meat our needs as well as to the needs of the forest for its own maintenance;
2. Damage to forest can be reduced by encouraging and educating for sustainable management of areas, such as discouraging shifting cultivation and promotion of forest products as medicinal plants, dyes, fishers, gums, resins, fodders, bamboo among the local people. Involve the local people in the prevention of poaching;
3. Encouragement of Ecotourism, which is one way of forest use and means to conservation. Ecotoursim provides first hand participation and encourages recognition by everyone, involved of the value of resource;
4. People should be encouraged to invest in the future of the land by giving them access to resources. Traditional methods of cultivation, forestry, and agro forestry increase biodiversity. Hence these should be promoted.

People should use compost and green manures to increase the fertility of soil. Mixed cropping should be encouraged;

5. Sacred groves are one of the best examples of preservation of biodiversity. Sacred groves are set up by local people under various religious believes. These sites being well preserved and provide shelter to many wild animals;
6. Establishment of protected areas and national parks and botanical gardens to provide protection to endangered species and thereby to preserve biodiversity;
7. Rehabilitate and restore degraded ecosystems and promote the recovery of threatened species. Local people should involve in carrying restoration activity;
8. A global publicity campaign is necessary to raise general consciousness of the value and importance of biodiversity and what its loss can mean to individuals and to the society. NGOs are already active in tackling environmental issues. The IUCN (International Union for Conservation of Nature and Natural Resources), World Wildlife Fund (WWF) and other organisation could also take part in this programme;
9. Public demonstration should be staged to draw the attention of policy makers to the problems arising out like hunger, population pressure, shortage of raw materials and environmental degradation;
10. Training programmes should be organised for academicians, taxonomists, administrators, forester geneticits, agronomists in particular and common man in general on resources management and conservation of biodiversity;
11. Make time-to-time environmental impact assesment with public participation or projects such as dams or resorvoires or hydroelectric plant construction that threatens biodiversity;
12. Stringent international and national laws should be formulated and implemented against the destruction of

natural habitats and for the protection of flora and fauna in the wild.

Important dates related to conservation of biodiversity:

1. Animal Welfare Fortnight - from 14th January.
2. Wildlife Week - first week of October.
3. World Forestry Day - 21st March.
4. World Animal Day - 3rd October.
5. World Habitat Day - 4th October.
6. World Environment Day - 5th June.
7. Biological Diversity Day - 29th December.

Measures in India

In India, at present biodiversity is being accorded a serious consideration through various acts, boards, institutes and reserves. These are:

1. India Board of Wildlife 1991;
2. The Wildlife Protection Act 1972 and Amendment Bill 1991;
3. The Forest Act 1980;
4. Biosphere Reserves;
5. Biodiversity Act 2002. Later Biological Diversity Rules 2004 were formulated. According to this act any one who destroys biodiversity without approval of authorities is liable to be imprisoned for two years or to pay a fine of Rs. 1000000;
6. Establishment of National Parks, Sancturies Projects for Wild Animals;
7. National Bureau of Plant Genetic Resources, New Delhi;
8. National Bureau of Animal Genetic Resources, Karnal;
9. National Bureau of Fish Genetic Resources, Lucknow;
10. Wildlife Institute of India;
11. In India at present there are 448 sanctuaries, 85 national parks and 10 biosphere reserves;
12. Under the world heritage convention, 5 natural sites in India have been declared as world heritage site;

13. A potential example of an highly endangered in India is the *panthera tigries* it is estimated that India had about 40000 tigers in 1900 and the number declined to 1800 in 1972. Hence project tiger was launched in 1973. Project elephant was launched in 1992.

Conclusion

An integrated approach is necessary for conserving the global biodiversity. Conservation must be closely coupled with socio-economic development especially in those countries where mounting human pressure threatens the very existence of mankind.

Man could not go extinct like the Dinosaurs due to an ice age, or asteroid collision or evolutionary pressure; he would become extinct because of his own insensitivity to nature. One day may be someone will write on epitaph for man:

"He Dug His Own Grave".

References

1. Agrobios Newsletter, Vol. No. 1, Issue No. 9, 2003.
2. Agrobios Newsletter, Vol. No. 2, Issue No. 10, March 2004.
3. Agrobios Newsletter, Vol. No. 2, Issue No. 9, February 2004.
4. Science Reporter, August 2004.
5. Environmental Studies—Binapani Satpathy and Amiya Dash, 2nd Edition, 2005.
6. Text Book of Environmental Studies by Nigar Alam 1st Edition, 2003.
7. Environmental Studies by Ajaya Kumar Patro, 1st Edition, 1997.
8. Dines Objective Biology, August 2003.
9. Rudra Dutt and K.P.M. Sundharam, Indian, Economy, 1998.
10. The Hindu Survey of the Environment, 1993.
11. Environmental Conservation Movement, Orissa 3rd Edition, 1993.
12. The Journal of Environmental Science, Orissa Environmental Society Vol. 3, No. 1, June 1990.

3

ROLE OF EDUCATION AND ECOLOGICAL CONSERVATION FOR A SUSTAINABLE SOCIETY *A GENERAL OUTLOOK*

Dr. Santosh Kumar Pradhan *

Premananda Pradhan **

Introduction

We are living in a critical juncture of human history, under the shadow of ethnic warfare, nuclear saber rattling and an essentially discriminating economic regime. Sc that the crux of the present world order is the issue of ecology, development and gender issues. Among all these issues, environmental issue has gained primacy in recent discourses.

The world is plagued with a series of natural calamities such as soil erosion, ecological degradation and extinction of sustainable biodiversity. It has been observed and experienced that there is huge losses of ecological conservation. This is due to the lack of awareness, literacy and unconsciousness of the rural folk. In this context igniting the level of education in the minds of the rural communities ecological conservation could be possible.

Biodiversity *Vs.* Education

The variety of plant and animal species is essential for human survival. The protection and conservation of the diverse range of species of animal and plant life and their habitats is the aim of the United Nations convention on biological diversity,

* Keen Researcher on Socio-economic Issues Associated with S.P.S.P., B. Berhampur, Kachakhandi, Ganjam.

** UGC Research Fellow, Aska Science College, Aska.

to which 180 states are parties. The convention obligates states to conserve biodiversity, ensure its sustainable development and provide for the fair equitable sharing of benefits from the use of genetic resources.

Importance of Education

Education is a fundamental human right, it not only proceeding the developing structure of human being but also rectified the spiritual gaining all stage. Without education life is meaningless. Education brought each and every processes development of qualitative human being in all time. The emerging of international concern like, global acidification, global warming, deforestation and ozone depletion are control through the process of education. It recognises the goal of the survival of human species, of the realisation of an acceptable quality of life for each human being in present and future civilisation.

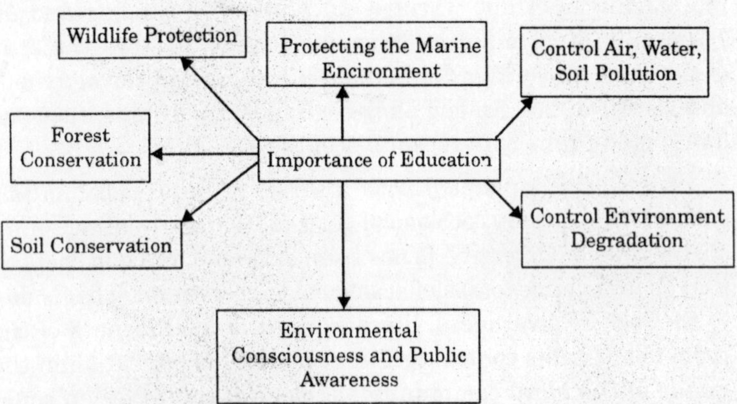

The related work of the organisation emphasised natural resources exploration and utilisation shown escalating alarm over the impact of development on ecology of the plant and human well-being is also rectified through the education. Education also changing the human behaviour by utilised proper method for what to produce, how to produce, how much to consume for maintainable the ecological conservation. It also works for the process of rectification, justification and implementation for ecological conservation. It teach the human being at the early childhood for “save nature leave pleasure”

more plantation with controlling the deforestation, soil erosion, creating free pollution zone upon the air, water, soil through the process of scientific research orientation. So in this manner importance of education and ecological conservation is inter-related, without education nothing is possible for survivable human being happy and pleasure. The importance of education for ecological conservation is also reflected the above chart.

Demographic Profile of Wild Population in South Ghumusar Forest Zone

Bhetanai, Balipadar or Buguda comes under the jurisdiction of south Ghumusar. To justified the research analysis about the wildlife conservation zone, Bhetanai wildlife conservation zone has been purposively selected. Bhetanai is situated about 10 kms from the block headquarter of Aska. The natural surrounding and ecological environment is considered a life supportive climate for wild animals and spices. It is perhaps the vertiable darling of Ganjam district, it is a safe haven for blackbucks. The people of these locality are highly sensitised so far as the wildlife conservation and eco-management is concerned. For the protection of the blackbucks a Management Committee has been formed. This is known as "BBMC" (Blackbuck Management Committee). Table 3.1 depicts the real statistic relating to the villages where blackbucks are found (*See Table on next page*). Table 3.2 depicts the profile of wild population in the state of Orissa including the types and numbers of wild species. (*See Table on page 47*)

Ganjam a Safe Haven for Blackbucks

This place (Bhetonai) is highly safety and considered as a safe haven for blackbucks, so that a large influx of blackbucks are residing here.

People's Attitude for Wildlife Conservation

There is a very old and strong tradition of protecting the blackbucks in a cluster of about 50 villages in Bhetonai-Balipadar-Buguda are of Ganjam District. These villagers believe that the presence of Blackbucks in their crop fields brings good harvest and prosperity to the village. Blackbucks are found freely roaming in these villages and the people bear with them when they eat away their standing crop of paddy, cereals or vegetables.

Table 3.1 Detail of Villages where Blackbuck is Seen

Sl. No.	*Name of the Range*	*Name of the CD Block*	*Name of the Gram Panchayat*	*Name of Village*
1	*2*	*3*	*4*	*5*
1.		Aska	Babanpur	Babanpur
2.		Aska	Pandiapathar	Naryanpur
3.		Aska	Pandiapathar	Pandiapathar
4.		Aska	Sidhanai	Sidhanai
5.		Aska	Sidhanai	Banabali
6.		Kabisurya Nagar	Subalaya	Nachunibadi
7.		Kabisurya Nagar	Kaniari	Madhiapalli
8.		Aska	Kharia	Sahibbagada
9.		Aska	Kharia	Kharia
10.	Aska Range	Aska	Bhetnoi	Charimaili
11.		Aska	Bhetnoi	Bhetnoi
12.		Buguda	Badakholi	Dhanija
13.		Aska	Babanpur	Sahapur
14.		Aska	Babanpur	Dhunkuni
15.		Aska	Bhetanai	Dasanapalli
16.		Aska	Badagaon	Dhunpalli
17.		Aska	Pandiapathar	Bhejiput
18.		Aska	Bhetanai	Bajrakote
19.		Aska	Bhetanai	Sandhi Nuapalli
20.	Buguda Range	Buguda	Kalamba	Gahangu
21.		Buguda	Balipadar	Balipadar
22.		Buguda	Kalamba	Kalamba
23.		Buguda	Badakholi	Badakholi
24.		Buguda	Badakholi	Sanakholi
25.		Buguda	Antarapada	Pratap Dhananjayapur
26.		Buguda	Arakhapur	Mahulapalli
27.		Buguda	Kholokhali	Ramagada
28.		Buguda	Solundi	Thanapali
29.		Buguda	Buguda	Ramanda
30.		Buguda	Golabandha	Subudhipalli
31.		Buguda	Kholokhali	Kholokhali
32.		Buguda	NAC Buguda	Kanjiapalli

(Contd...)

1	*2*	*3*	*4*	*5*
33.		Buguda	Kholokhali	Laxmipur
34.		Buguda	NAC Buguda	Golamundula
35.		Buguda	Golabandha	Betarsingi
36.		Buguda	Kholokhali	Talasakar
37.		Buguda	Belapur	Belapur
38.		Buguda	Antarapada	Antarapada
39.		Buguda	Pangidi	Pangidi
40.		Buguda	Pangidi	Tikarapada
41.		Buguda	Pangidi	Manikapur
42.		Buguda	A. Karadabadi	Dengapadar
43.		Buguda	Motabadi	Dakarabadi
44.		Buguda	Bhamasiali	Chadhiapali
45.		Buguda	Bhamasiali	Bhamasiali
46.		Jagannath Prasad	Udayapur	Udayapur
47.		Jagannath Prasad	Panchubhuti	Panchubhuti
48.		Jagannath Prasad	Kumpapada	Lunidhepa
49.		Jagannath Prasad	Kumpapada	Kanachai
50.		Jagannath Prasad	Kumpapada	Kumpapada

Table 3.2 Wild Population in the State

Sl. No.	*Name of species*	*Number*	*Year*	*Remarks*
1.	Tiger	194	1998	In the wild (entire state)
2.	Leopard	401	1998	In the wild (entire state)
3.	Elephant	1872	1999	In the wild (entire state)
4.	Salt Water Crocodile	672	1998	Bhitarkanika
5.	Birds	14.33 lakh	1999	Chilika Lake
6.	Dolphin	79	1998	Chilika Lake
7.	Blackbuck	786	2004	Balipadar-Bhetanai wildlife reserve

Source: Chief Warden, Wildlife, Orissa, Bhubaneswar.

Their numbers have risen from 551 in 1998 to 786 in 2004, and there is no record of any killing of these free living animals in this area in many many years. These villagers have also been actively helping the local forest officials in preventing poaching by outsiders. They have also often come forward to provide veterinary care to any black buck when it is injured. The values of tolerance and compassion for a wild animal species have been ingrained in the minds of each of these villagers, who have now formed a 'Blackbuck Management Committee'. These villages have set an example in coexistence between man and wild animal in the best traditions of "*Vasudheva Kutumbakam*"; and their committee is a torch bearer of this ideal.

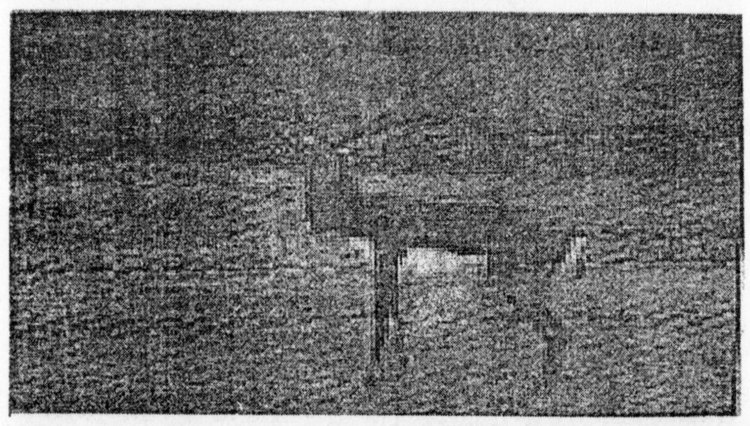

These animals are in the same family as Nilgai and Chousingha. They are different from deer as they do not shed their horns. Blackbuck is considered to be the second fastest animal in the world next only to Cheetah. There has been very fast decline in the population of this throughout our country.

It has been accorded the highest protection status by being included in the Schedule-I of the Wildlife (Protection) Act. It is also in the endangered animals list as per the IUCN Red Data Book.

In recognition of the outstanding contribution to the cause of protection of wild animals, and to the larger cause of spreading the wildlife conservation ethos, this committee representing the 50 villages has been selected from among 9 nominations for being honoured with the 'Biju Patnaik award for wildlife conservation' for the year 2004-05.

Education and Sustainable Society

Education is the supreme hallmark of any social change. It expands our mental horizon, supports our intellectual development. Therefore, there is a positive co-relation between education and any developmental effort.

In order to promote awareness for environmental protection and conservation, environment education and awareness promotion should be encouraged. If people would be consciousness about their eco-surroundings with self-interest, then we can establish a sustainable society. The shortages of present as well as for the future generation could be mitigated. Environment as a public goods, therefore, protection of the environment from all types of pollution and eco-hazards is the risk and responsibilities of all citizen. Developing the environmental consciousness should be top priority of any organisations including GOs and NGOs. Our State Government have instituted "Prakruti Mitra" and "Prakruti Bandhu" awards for encouraging voluntary organisations/ villages/ institutions and individuals.

4

COMMUNITY PARTICIPATION AND SUSTAINABLE DEVELOPMENT A FOCUS

Premananda Pradhan* *

Dr. L.R. Patro**

In the present day world we are in the grip of environmental problems, which was never experienced earlier. In every corner of this planet, there is palpable concern about the specter of the environmental crisis. While the rich and well-off talk about ozone layer depletion, global warming, climatic change, nuclear hazards, urban congestion and air, water and noise pollution, the poor man only understands his crops whither in parched land, and his wife walks five kilometers or more daily to collect water fuel, wood and fodder. Since environment as a public good and satisfies the principle of non-excludability, its protection is highly indispensable. Thus, in this context, peoples, participation in protecting the environment is necessary.

Peoples' participation in a broader sense means their total involvement with development agencies in deciding the programmes and activities, fixing of priorities, taking initiative and carrying out the programme as partners by the contribution of their ideas, interest, material, money, labour and time.

---

* Research Fellow, UGC Sponsored Major Project, College Square, Aska, P.O. Kotinada, District Ganjam, Orissa-761111. E-Mail: premananda 1975@sify.com

** Laboratory of Environmental Toxicology, Department of Zoology, Kshetrabasi DAV Science College, Nirakarpur 761111, Orissa (India) E-mail: dr.lrpatro@rediffmail.com, dr.lingarajpatro@sify.com. Mobile: 09337739823

All the development programmes of various departments revolve around people contributing to their socio-economic development. Therefore, through flexible planning and implementation, usage of indigenous technologies, creating awareness among the people is the pre-requisite elements of sustainable environment development. Due to environmental pollution and ecological degradation, today, man suffers from untold miseries and natural disasters such as flood, famine, drought, cyclone and global warming etc. Therefore, sensitising the gender and involving the people through Self Help Groups (SHGs), these recurring problems can be mitigated and the habitat destruction, the flora and fauna of the country can be protected and the conducive environment can be emerged.

In this paper a scholastic presentation has been done pertaining to the causes of environmental degradation and its adverse consequences and its solution through active peoples participation.

Objectives of the Paper

The main objectives of the paper are:

(*i*) To find out the alarming indicators of environmental disasters;

(*ii*) What does sustainable development mean?

(*iii*) Is sustainable development is the key to survival?

(*iv*) Why peoples' participation is necessary ?

(*v*) To suggest some policy options to strengthen the people's participation making the development sustainable.

In the beginning, man lived in harmony with nature, but as his numbers grew and his scientific discoveries and inventions led him on the path of industrialisation, he became the predator and his increasing demands on the environment and its resources have led to its exploitation and degradation. Therefore, participation of the people in the process of development is the need of the hour. Peoples' participation evolve around three pivotal points such as: (1) Effective networking in the village for dissemination of information; (2) Equal opportunity for all in the village for expressing their opinion; (3) institutional support for implementation of projects, according to UNIDS. (1977)

Participation is meaningless unless active, observes Lalitha Nataraj (1986) popular participation, as a process, can be defined as active and meaning full involvement of the mass of people at different levels. First, in the decision making process for the determination of the social goals and allocation of resources to achieve them, and second, in the voluntary execution of resulting projects and programmes. It is the decision making of the community as an essential and ingredient of participation.

People's participation in the process of development can be shown the following flow chart:

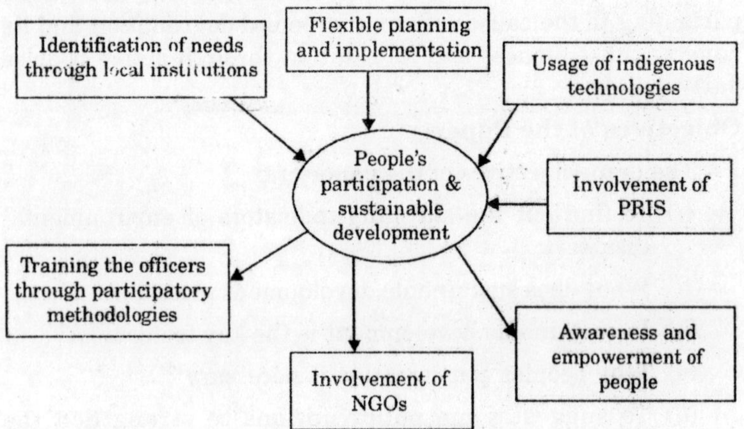

The Concept of Sustainable Development

In the primitive days people were unaware regarding the adverse impact of depletion of natural resources. Now man could realise that the depletion of natural resources has brought unprecedented havoc such as global warming, ecological imbalance, depletion of ozone layer and other environmental crisis such as soil erosion, uncertain in rainfall pollution: air, water, noise etc. Therefore, man could become cautious about the present as well as for the future generations.

The emergence of sustainable development is now a matter of valuable discourse in recent time. Today the environment is experienced with a few alarming indicators which are listed below:

(1) About 1.5 billion hectares of land was lost as degraded and deemed for crops;

(2) The non-agricultural uses of precious arable land for townships, parks, air strips, car parks etc is accounted at 0.1 to 0.2 hectares per person;

(3) Only 35 per cent of world's crops are produced from 15 per cent of available irrigated area;

(4) The water table descended by 80 feet Bangkok and in Tamilnadu by 100 feet, since 1958;

(5) India loses three per cent of forests per annum and hence, India's areas of degraded land are largest in the world.

The world commission on environment and development (1987), considered sustainable development as the ability to meet the needs of the present generation without compromising the ability of the future generations to meet their needs. Sustainable development cannot be discussed in isolation; it has to be discussed as a function of other socio-demographic factors, *viz.* population, natural resources dependence, socio-demographic pressure, poverty and institutional establishment. An economy is said to be sustainable if and only it is dynamically efficient and the resulting stream of maximised total welfare function is non-declining over time.

Sustainability of the project requires reflection of peoples" needs, expectations etc., which can be tapped only through bottom up approach in planning process. Hence, peoples' participation is a kind of ignition for programme identification, fuel for implementing the programme and thus an essential component for successful of development programme.

Sustainable Development: Key to Survival

According to an annual report "State of the world" prepared by "world watch", as a result of our population size, consumption patterns and technology choices, we have suppressed the planet's carrying capacity. Human demands are approaching the limits of oceanic fisheries to supply fish, of lands to support livestock and the hydrological cycle to produce fresh water. Besides, increasingly polluted water bodies are causing drinking water shortages in the urban town's and metropolitan cities. Therefore, now it is the responsibility of the entire global community to work honestly for the environmental protection to save Mother Nature from any disaster.

Getting peoples' participation in any developmental programmes is not an easy task. There must be a good political will. It means when all types of people belong to different categories, must involve in the matters of programme implementation execution and decision making etc. However, peoples' participation as a catalytic agent in the process of development is to meaningless. For instance, in West-Bengal over a two decades, a single political party is dominating in the matters of administration. Other people are not allowed to take active participation. Therefore, peoples' participation is meaningful if all the people are involved in the developmental activities without any barriers.

To make people's participation strong and active, the following suggestive strategies are directed:

(*i*) Identification of needs through local institutions;

(*ii*) Flexible planning and implementation;

(*iii*) Awareness and empowerment of people;

(*iv*) Involvement of PRIs;

(*v*) Involvement of NGOs;

(*vi*) Gender sensitisation in the methods of peoples, participation.

References

1. *World Commission on Environment and Development : Our Common Future,* Oxford University Press (1987).
2. People's Participation for Sustainable Development, Reddy, Dr. M.R., Rajanikanth and *Yojana*, April 1998.
3. "Protecting the Environment from the Disaster" Banarjee, S. *Kurukshetra*, Dec 1995.
4. Sustainable Development : Concept and Measurement, Singh, Kultarr *Kurukshetra*, Jan 2005.
5. *Edu Tracks,* February 2005, Vol. 4 No.6
6. *Rural Development and Social Change,* NIRD Volume (ed) R.R. Prasad and G. Rajanikanth Foundation Day Series.

5

TOXICITY OF VANADIUM
AN ULTRA TRACE ELEMENT

Azzam Ali, S. Sudha
and B.V. Venkataraman*

Early History

Vanadium is a natural element in the earth. It is a white to grey metal, often found as crystals. Vanadium occurs naturally in fuel oils and coal. Nils Gabriel Sefstrom, a Swedish Chemist, was the first person recognised vanadium compound as a new metal in 1831. The attractive beautiful multi-colours of vanadium prompted him to name the new metal after "Vanadis", the legendary Norse Goddess of Beauty. Subsequently, the mineral was called vanadinite (Hudson 1964). Due to its wide use in industrial processes as a catalyst, the concentration of vanadium is increasing in the atmosphere. The physiological effects of vanadium were studied long before its current renaissance. As early as 1876, John Priestly of Manchester reported on the physiological action of vanadium in frogs, pigeons, guinea pigs, rabbits, dogs, and cats. Some of his conclusions are still valid today. For example, there is a poisonous effect on the introduction of a soluble salt (vanadate) into the system via the stomach or direct injection into veins. In 1877, Larmuth followed John Priestly's work concerning the toxicity of the various known vanadium forms. The pharmacological value of metavanadate was recognised a century ago in France and it was acclaimed as "Panacee Universelle" for many chronic ailments. In 1899, at the turn of the century vanadium was widely used for therapeutic purposes in France for the treatment of anaemia, tuberculosis, chronic rheumatism and diabetes. In order to increase appetite, strength and weight, up to 5 mg/day of sodium metavanadate

* Department of Pharmacology, St. John's Medical College, Bangalore–560034, Karnataka.

was taken orally (Hudson 1964). A tonic (neogade) containing a small quantity of metavanadate, based on an original French formulation was available in the Indian market. Most food material used for human consumption contains vanadium—no more than 0.1 μg/g of food. Accessory food items such as black pepper, tealeaf, cocoa powder, tobacco, and mushrooms contain vanadium in μg/g concentrations (Nechay 1984). Dietary supplement of vanadate will increase its tissue content, which is stored in a non-toxic form. The importance of vanadium as a powerful inhibitor of the sodium pump was recognised after it was found to be the active inhibitor present in the samples of crystalline ATP derived from horse muscle but not in yeast or synthetic samples (Cantley *et al.*, 1978a).

Chemistry

Metallic vanadium does not occur in nature. Vanadium, a greyish ductile metal, is easily combustible and at high concentration, it may form an explosive mixture with air. Metallic vanadium reacts with oxygen, nitrogen and carbon at a relatively low temperature (< 300°C). It forms oxidative states of 1^-, 0, 2^+, 3^+, 4^+ and 5^+, the last four being the most common. Of these, the trivalent (3^+) state is unstable at physiological pH, undergoes rapid oxidation, and picks up O_2 to form peroxovanadate (5^+ state). Vanadium in the 3^+ oxidation state (vanadium trioxide V_2O_3) is basic and dissolves in acid forming a green hexa-aquo ion.

In solution vanadium in the 3^+ state is a strong reducing agent and slowly attacks water with the production of hydrogen:

$$2V^{+++} + 2H_2O \longleftrightarrow 2V^{++++} + 2OH^- + H_2$$

Oxidation State 4^+ is considered the less toxic storage form (Macara 1980). It is stable in acid pH as the blue vanadyl cation that is not easily oxidised (Shi and Dalai 1993) and is not capable of generating superoxide on auto-oxidation (Kalyani and Ramasarma 1992) as often presumed (Liochev and Fridovich 1990). It can be oxidised by H_2O_2 (Brooks and Sicillo 1971) and also by cytochrome C (Kalyani and Ramasarma 1992) and generates vanadate (5^+) and peroxo-complexes with the release of oxygen.

Vanadium in the 5^+ state (vanadium pentoxide V_2O_5) is the most common commercial form of vanadium. Vanadium pentoxide is used as a catalyst in many oxidation reactions and may be prepared in special forms for this purpose. It dissolves in water and acids and forms vanadates with bases. Pentavalent vanadium (5^+ state) compounds exist as monomers (ortho- and meta-forms), dimers (V_2) and tetramers (V_4) Vanadate polymerises to a cage-like structure of a decamer (V_{10}) gaining a golden yellow colour. Chemical reactions of vanadium are similar to those of phosphorus in many respects. Vanadate forms polynuclear species with phosphate. The V-O bonds are longer than the P-O bonds and this is the basis for the high competitiveness of vanadate in phosphate ester hydrolysis (Macara 1980). Organic compounds of vanadium are generally unstable (Weast 1987). The following table lists the physical properties of vanadium and some compounds:

Vanadium and Some Compounds

Compounds	*Forms*	*Colour*	*MP (°C)*	*BP (°C)*	*Water solubility*
Vanadium	Metal	Grey	1890	3380	Insoluble
Vanadium pentoxide	Crystal	Yellow or Red	690	1750	0.7
Vanadium trioxide	Crystal	Black	1970	—	Slight
Sodium meta vanadate	Crystal	Colourless or green	630	—	211
Vanadium tetra chloride	Liquid	Red/Brown	28	148.5	Reacts
Vanadyl sulphate	Crystal	Bluish Green	—	—	Soluble
Decavanadate	Crystal	Yellow Orange	—	—	Soluble

Vanadium is mostly combined with other metals to make special metal mixtures called alloys. Vanadium in the form of vanadium oxide is a component in special kinds of steel that is used for automobile parts, springs, and ball bearings. Small amounts of vanadium are used in making rubber, plastics, ceramics, and other chemicals.

Potential for Human Exposure

Vanadium mainly enters the environment from natural sources and from the burning of fuel oils. It stays in the air, water, and soil for a long time. It does not dissolve well in water.

It combines with other elements and particles. It sticks to soil sediments. Low levels have been found in plants, but it is not likely to build up in the tissues of animals.

The general population is exposed to background levels of vanadium primarily through ingestion of food (about 10-20 micrograms daily). Workers in industries processing or using vanadium compounds are commonly exposed to higher than background levels via the inhalation pathway. Exposure through inhalation may also be of importance in urban areas where large amounts of residual fuel oil are burnt. Other populations possibly exposed to higher than background levels include those ingesting foodstuffs contaminated by vanadium-enriched soil, fertilisers, or sludge. Populations in the vicinity of vanadium-containing hazardous waste sites may also be exposed to higher than background levels.

Vanadium in Biological Systems

Vanadium is an ultra trace metal, present in mammalian tissues at concentrations below 1 μM (Nechay, 1984). The assay of vanadium in biological experiments is crucial to understand the role of this metal in biology. Vanadium is found in the urine of exposed workers. This measurement is specific for vanadium. Some vanadium workers develop a characteristic green tongue, as a result of direct accumulation of the vanadium dust on the tongue. Vanadium content in biological samples may be estimated by various methods such as atomic absorption spectrometry, neutron activation analysis, inductively coupled plasma, dc arc emission, dc plasma atomic emission spectroscopy, mass spectroscopy, mass spectrometry, spectrophotometry, energy dispensive X-ray fluorescence and electron paramagnetic resonance (Martin and Chasteen 1988). However, it is often useful to be able to specifically measure vanadium concentrations in a given oxidation state by chemical assay. N-benzoyl-N-phenylhydroxylamine is a specific reagent for vanadium-V and can be used to assay V^{5+} in biological samples (Priyadarshini and Tandon 1961). A quantitative enzyme assay procedure for determining the amounts of V^{5+} and V^{4+} in biological samples has been developed based on vanadium inhibition of alkaline or acid phosphatases (Crans *et al.*, 1990).

Micro-organisms

Vanadium is essential for the mould *Aspergillus niger* (Bertrand 1942) and the green algae *Scenedesmus obliquus* (Arnon and Wessel 1953; Arnon 1958). It may play a role in photosynthesis in the latter. The yeast *Candida slooffii* at high temperatures (Roitman *et al.,* 1969) has shown a need for vanadium. The growth effects of vanadium in Azotobacter and other bacteria have been related to the ability of vanadium, in lieu of molybdenum, to catalyse nitrogen fixation reactions (Horner *et al.,* 1942; Takahashi and Nasoǹ 1957).

Animals

Vanadium deficiency has been reported in chicks (Hopkins and Mohr 1971; Nielsen and Ollerich 1973) and rats (Schwarz and Milne 1971) and vanadium is considered essential for these animals (Underwood 1977; Vouk 1979; Nechay 1984). Hopkins and Mohr (1974) observed reduced feather growth in chickens. They also reported impaired reproduction due to decreased fertility and increased perinatal mortality in rats fed a low vanadium diet (10 μmol/kg) over four generations.

Nielsen and Ollerich (1973) carried out further studies on chicks and rats giving different types of low-vanadium experimental diets to examine the effects of vanadium deficiency. In rats, vanadium deficiency adversely affected prenatal survival, growth, physical appearance, haematocrit, plasma-cholesterol levels and hepatic lipid and phospholipid levels. In chicks, low vanadium intake produced adverse effects on growth, feathering, haematocrit, bone development, and plasma-cholesterol levels. However, consistent deficiency effects were not observed in chicks or rats in any of the studies.

Vanadates appear to have an insulin-like action (Heyliger *et al.,* 1985). In female Wistar rats made diabetic with streptozotocin (55 mg/kg iv) and given sodium orthovanadate in the drinking water at a concentration of 0.6-0.8 mg/ml for 4 weeks, the serum insulin level was low, but there was no increase in blood-glucose levels compared with controls. In diabetic rats not treated with vanadate, serum insulin levels were also low, but blood glucose levels were increased 3-fold. The cardiac performance of vanadium-treated animals did not differ significantly from that of non-diabetic controls. It was concluded that vanadate controlled blood glucose levels and prevented the decline in cardiac performance due to diabetes. The results of *in vitro* studies suggest that vanadium may play a specific physiological role as a regulator of the sodium pump (Macara 1980). Vanadate has been shown to inhibit Na^+, K^+-ATPase in intact human red blood cells (Rifkin 1965; Cantley *et al.,* 1977, 1978a, b). It also has potent diuretic and natriuretic effects in rats (Balfour *et al.,* 1978; Westenfelder *et al.,* 1981). It was considered a powerful inhibitor of Na^+, K^+-ATPase in the microsomal fractions of the kidney, brain and heart in several species, including human beings. Mg^{2+}–ATPase was up to 10,000 times more resistant to vanadium inhibition than Na^+, K^+–ATPase (Nechay and Saunders 1978).

Similarly, *in vivo* studies on laying chickens fed calcium orthovanadate (Dose 0.25-100 mg/kg) for 15 months showed inhibition of Na^+, K^+-ATPase activity in the kidney (Phillips *et al.,* 1982). The inhibition of Na^+, K^+-ATPase by vanadate can be reversed by catecholamines, though these do not have any effects on the activity in the absence of vanadate (Hudgins and Bond 1979). The inhibition is also partially prevented by the reducing agents, ascorbic acid and glutathione (Grantham and Glynn 1979). The mechanism by which cells reduce cytoplasmic vanadium^{5+} to vanadium^{4+} was investigated using human red blood cells (Macara *et al.,* 1980). The authors concluded that vanadate is reduced by cytoplasmic glutathione and this explains the resistance of the Na^+, K^+-ATPase to vanadium in intact cells. Since vanadate (V^{5+}) is a potent inhibitor of Na^+, K^+-ATPase, many physiological and biochemical processes are vanadium sensitive (Grantham 1980; Nechay 1984). For example vanadium compounds inhibit phosphorylase, ribonuclease, adenylate kinase, phosphofructokinase, squalene synthetase, glyceraldehyde-3-phosphate dehydrogenase (Macara 1980), glucose-6-phosphatase (Singh *et al.,* 1981) and phosphotyrosyl-protein-phosphatase (Swarup *et al.,* 1982).

The membrane neutral (K^+) p-nitrophenylphosphatase in the fraction of skeletal muscle was inhibited by vanadium^{4+} to vanadium^{5+} (Vyskocil *et al.,* 1981). In higher concentrations vanadium (10^{-5} to 10^{-3}M) even potentiated the hyperpolarization of the muscle fibres (Zemkova *et al.*, 1982) probably by increasing the intracellular potassium level. These findings have led to the hypothesis that vanadate could control sodium pump activity *in vivo,* perhaps via a vanadium^{4+}: vanadium^{5+} equilibrium connecting pump activity to the cellular state. However, vanadate in the red cell is reduced to vanadium^{4+}, which then binds to haemoglobin (Cantley and Aisen 1979), a reaction that seems to be essentially quantitatively driven by glutathione (Macara *et al.*, 1980), NADH (Vyskocil *et al.* 1981), or by other mild reducing agents such as ascorbate or norepinephrine. The role of the vanadium^{4+}: vanadium^{5+} redox equilibrium in the regulation of cation flow across cell membranes has yet to be precisely demonstrated.

Absorption

The absorption and distribution of vanadium compounds depends on the route of entry and the solubility of the compounds in the fluids. The solubility of vanadium in biological media varies (Reznik 1954). The following compounds are listed in decreasing order of solubility: (*a*) in gastric juice: vanadyl sulphate: sodium vanadate, ammonium vanadate and vanadium pentoxide; (*b*) in blood serum and in 0.22 per cent sodium carbonate solution: sodium vanadate, ammonium vanadate, vanadium pentoxide, and vanadyl sulphate. The higher the solubility in water and biological media, the more toxic the compound, presumably because of better absorption (Roshchin 1968). Soluble vanadium compounds, inhaled and deposited in the lung, are readily absorbed. It has been estimated that about 25 per cent of soluble vanadium compounds may be absorbed via the respiratory tract (ICRP 1960). Absorption from the respiratory tract was demonstrated in workers exposed to vanadium dust, who showed increased concentrations of vanadium in the urine (Lewis 1959; Gylseth *et al.*, 1979; Maroni *et al.*, 1983). In general, vanadium salts are poorly absorbed from the human gastrointestinal tract. The International Commission on Radiological Protection (ICRP 1960) estimates for the gastrointestinal absorption of soluble vanadium compounds is 2 per cent. A low degree of absorption was also found by Roshchin *et al.*, (1980). Though dermal absorption has been reported in animal studies, according to USEPA (1977), the skin appears to be a minor route of vanadium uptake for human beings. In an *in vitro* study using V^{48} radiotracer, there was no penetration of human skin samples (Roshchin 1980).

Distribution and Biotransformation

Absorbed vanadium is transported mainly in the plasma (Schroeder *et al.,* 1963; Ordhzonikidze *et al.,* 1977; Roshchin *et al.,* 1980). Highest concentrations tend to occur in the liver, kidney, and lung. It is mainly stored in fat and serum lipids (Schroeder *et al.,* 1963). Owing to low gastrointestinal absorption, ingested vanadium is predominantly eliminated unabsorbed in the faeces. The main route of excretion is through the kidneys. The ratio of amounts eliminated in the urine and faeces is 5:1 (Talvitie and Wagner 1954). In animal studies Mitchell and Floyd (1954) showed that ascorbic acid increases the elimination of vanadium in both urine and faeces. Vanadium in tissues, such as bone is released slowly.

Effects on Organisms in the Environment

The growth of an aquatic plant is stimulated by trace quantities of vanadium (1-10 μg/l), but concentrations above 100 μg/l are toxic. Some marine invertebrates, such as the tunicates, accumulate vanadium levels up to 0.3 per cent dry weight. Invertebrates are generally less sensitive to vanadium (9-day LC_{50} values in the range of 10-65 mg/l) than fish (4-6 day LC_{50} values in the range of 0.5-22 mg/l). The pH is an important modulator of vanadium toxicity. Vanadium in soils at concentrations of 10 mg/kg or more is toxic for terrestrial plants.

Effects on Experimental Animals

Vanadium compounds are acutely toxic by most routes of exposure, in most species. In general, the toxicity of vanadium compounds increases with the Oxidation State. The rabbit and guinea pig are more sensitive than the rat and mouse. Repeated administration of vanadium compounds produces changes in protein metabolism, lipid profile, enzyme activities, reproductive activities, and other metabolic actions. Due to poor absorption from the gastrointestinal tract, the metal is not very toxic for human beings when ingested.

Lethal doses of vanadium (mg V_2O_5/kg) in experimental animals

Compound	*Rabbit*	*Guinea-pig*	*Rat*	*Mouse*
Colloidal vanadium pentoxide	1-2	20-28	—	87.5-117.5
Ammonium metavanadate	1.5-2	1-2	20-30	25-30
Sodium orthovanadate	2-3	1 -2	50-60	50-100
Sodium pyrovanadate	3-4	1-2	40-50	50-100
Sodium tetravanadate	6-8	18-20	30-40	25-50
Sodium hexavanadate	30-40	40-50	40-50	100-150
Vanadyl sulphate	18-20	34-45	158-190	125-150

Effects on Human Beings

In the past, vanadium compounds were prescribed as therapeutic agents for anaemia, chlorosis, tuberculosis and diabetes. Vanadium was also used as an antiseptic, a spirochetocide and as a tonic. Clinical picture of poisoning shows a broad spectrum of toxic effects of vanadium on the respiratory, circulatory and central nervous systems, the digestive organs, kidneys, and skin. Vanadium poisoning in humans can be diagnosed on the basis of a history of exposure, the clinical picture, a green tongue (due to the hexa-aqua ion), and measurements of vanadium levels in blood cells, plasma and urine. The value of various tests of the secondary metabolic effects of poisoning is disputed.

The following figure (*see on next page*) summarises the existing information on health effects of inhalational, oral, and dermal exposure of humans and animals to vanadium and compounds (adapted from ATSDR, 1992):

Data are available from humans regarding acute, intermediate, and chronic inhalation exposure to vanadium pentoxide and on immunologic and neurologic effects, primarily from case studies of factory workers. Data regarding acute effects are available from volunteers who ingested ammonium vanadyl tartarate in capsules for intermediate periods. No human dermal data were located.

	Inhalation	*Oral*	*Dermal*
Death	Only animal data	Only animal data	—
Systemic Effects:			
Acute	Animal & Human data	Animal & Human data	—
Intermediate	Animal & Human data	Animal & Human data	—
Chronic	Animal & Human data	Only animal data	—
Immunologic	Animal & Human data	Only animal data	—
Neurologic	Animal & Human data		—
Developmental	—	Only animal data	—
Reproductive	—	Only animal data	—
Genotoxic	—	—	—
Cancer	—	—	—

Death. There are no reports of death in humans following inhalation, oral, or dermal exposure to vanadium.

Systemic Effects

Respiratory Effects: The only significant, clearly documented effect in humans is mild to moderate respiratory distress and mucosal irritation from exposure to vanadium dusts. These people have coughs, chest pains, sore throats, and irritated eyes, but the symptoms usually disappear soon after exposure ceases. The response is similar to that of an upper respiratory tract infection.

The mechanism of vanadium's effect on the respiratory system is similar to that of other metals. In vitro tests show that vanadium damages alveolar macrophages (Castranova *et al.*, 1984). It does this by decreasing the macrophage membrane integrity, thus impairing the cells' phagocytic ability and viability. Without macrophages, the respiratory system's ability to clear itself of many other particles normally found in the air is diminished.

Renal Effects: It is difficult to determine the potential for toxicity in humans. However, renal effects have not been observed upon urinalysis in occupationally exposed workers.

Immunological Effects: Very few data are available on the immunological effects of vanadium in humans. Cohen *et al.*, (1986) has suggested that the decreased macrophage phagocytic ability may explain why vanadium workers have increased susceptibility to respiratory disease.

Neurological Effects: Humans who have been exposed to vanadium dusts in the workplace have generally not reported significant effects related to the nervous systems. Some workers have reported non-specific effects such as dizziness or headaches. It is possible that the effects that vanadium has in inhibiting the sodium-potassium pump would adversely affect the nervous system but this has not been tested and/or reported. Vanadium does not accumulate in the brain of humans.

Developmental Effects: No direct information is available on developmental effects of vanadium in humans.

Reproductive Effects: Autopsy data have not provided detectable levels of vanadium in human reproductive organs. It is unlikely that the reproductive system is a sensitive indicator for vanadium toxicity in humans.

Genotoxic Effects: The only information on genotoxicity of vanadium is from in vitro studies (Kada *et al.,* 1980; Kanematsu *et al.,* 1980; Hanauske *et al.,* 1987). The majority of these studies show positive effects in test systems using bacteria, yeast, and mouse cells in culture for end points such as recombination repair, gene mutation, or DNA systems. None of these studies showed any indication of a cytotoxic effect. Human leukocytes have been shown to have DNA strand breaks from exposure to vanadate (Birnboim 1988). These in vitro data indicate that vanadium has the potential for genotoxicity in humans.

Cancer: No studies regarding the carcinogenicity of vanadium in humans were located. Workers who have been exposed to vanadium dusts did not show an increased number of cancer deaths (Orris *et al.,* 1983), although detailed studies were not performed.

Mitigation of Effects: Following oral exposure, dilution with water or milk is one way to decrease overall absorption (Stutz and Janus 1988). Induced emesis and gastric lavage are effective if performed soon after ingestion. To increase the excretion of the chemical, calcium disodium edentate and cathartic medication such as magnesium sulphate have been tried. If vanadium gets into the skin, washing the contaminated area with soapy water is recommended. For ocular exposure, it is suggested that the eyes by flushed with large amounts of saline or water. After acute inhalation exposure, pulmonary oedema may result, and oxygen administration may be necessary. Steroids such as prednisolone succinate or phthalate may prevent the development of a chemical lung oedema. Enhanced excretion of vanadium was achieved with chelation therapy provided by defroxamine mesylate (Gomez *et al.*, 1988). Dimercaprol and ascorbic acid may have value in the treatment of poisoning in human beings. There are no adequate epidemiological studies of mortality in occupationally exposed populations.

Conclusion

In 1985, a symposium was devoted to discuss the role of vanadium in Biology by FASEB (Nechay *et al* 1986). The International Programme on Chemical Safety (IPCS 1988), a joint venture of the United Nations Environment Programme (UNEP), the International Labour Organisation (ILO) and the World Health Organisation (WHO) published the meticulous work done on vanadium.

The Environmental Protection Agency requires discharges or spills of 1000 pounds or more of vanadium into the environment to be reported. The Occupational Safety and Health Administration has set an exposure limit of 0.05 milligrams per cubic meter for vanadium pentoxide dust and 0.1 mg/m^3 for vanadium pentoxide fumes in workplace air for an 8-hour workday, 40-hour workweek. The American Conference of Governmental Industrial Hygienists has recommended an occupational exposure limit of 0.05 mg/m^3 for vanadium pentoxide. The National Institute for Occupational Safety and Health has recommended that 35 mg/m^3 of vanadium be considered immediately dangerous to life and death. This is the exposure level of a chemical likely to cause permanent health problems or death.

There is lack of data on several aspects of the health effects of vanadium compounds. Confirmative mutagenicity and carcinogenicity studies are not consistent and they should be given high priority with long-term exposure studies. It is important to develop specific indicators for the detection of early adverse effects of vanadium on man.

Epidemiological studies on occupational hazards should be encouraged. This is an important aspect with regards to worker protection. There are considerable geographical variations in vanadium concentrations in air and water. Epidemiological studies on populations living in areas with high vanadium exposure should be carried out focusing on possible interactions with other pollutants.

References

Arnon, DI. (1958) The Role of Micronutrients in Plant Nutrition with Special Reference to Photosynthesis and Nitrogen Assimilation. In: Trace Elements. Ed. Lamb, CA., Bentley, OG., Beattie, JM. New York, Academic Press, 1-32.

Arnon, DI., Wessel, G. (1953) Vanadium as an Essential Element for Green Plants. Nature (Lond). 172:1039-1040.

ATSDR Agency for Toxic Substances and Disease Registry. (1992) Toxicological Profile for Vanadium and Compounds. Atlanta, GA: US Department of Health and Human Services, Public Health Service.

Balfour, WE., Grantham, J.J., Glynn, IM. (1978) Vanadate-stimulated Natriuresis. Nature (Lond). 275: 768p.

Bertrand, D. (1942) Le vanadium comme élément oligosynergique pour l'Aspergillus niger. Ann.lnst.Pasteur. 68: 226-244.

Birnboim , HC. (1988) A Superoxide Anion induced DNA Strand-break Metabolic Pathway in Human Leukocytes: Effects of Vanadate. Biochem Cell Biol. 66: 374-381.

Brooks, HB., Sicillio, F. (1971) Electron Spin Resonance Kinetic Studies of the Oxidation of Vanadium (IV) by Hydrogen Peroxide. Inorg. Chem. 10:2530-2534.

Cantley, LC. Jr., Canley, LG., Josephson, L. (1978a) A Characterisation of Vanadate Interactions with the (Na^+,K^+)-ATPase. J.Bio.Chem. 253: 7361-7368.

Cantley, LC. Jr., Aisen, P. (1979) The Fate of Cytoplasmic Vanadium. Implications on (Na^+, K^+ ATPase Inhibition. J. Biol. Chem. 254: 1781-1784.

Cantley, LC. Jr., Josephson, L., Warner, R., Yanagisawa, M.,Lechene, G., Guidotti, G. (1977) Vanadate is a Potent (Na^+,K^+)-ATPase Inhibitor Found in ATP Derived from Muscle. J. Bio.Chem. 252: 7421-7423

Cantley, LC.Jr., Resh, MD., Guidotti, G. (1978b) Vanadate Inhibits the Red Cell (Na^+, K^+)-ATPase from the Cytoplasmic Side. Nature. 272: 552-554.

Castranova, V., Bowman, L, Wright, JR., *et al.,* (1984) Toxicity of Metallic Ions in the Lung: Effects on Alveolar Macrophages and Alveolar Type II Cells. J. Toxicol. Environ. Health 13: 845-856.

Cohen, MD., Wei, Cl., Tan, H., *et al.,* (1986) Effect of Ammonium Metavanadate on the Murine Immune Response. J. Toxicol. Environ. Health 19: 279-298.

Crans, DC., Rithner, CD., Theisen, LA (1990) Application of Time Resolved 51V 2D NMR for Quantitation of Kinetic Exchange Pathways Between Vanadium Monomer, Dimmer, Tetramer, and Pentamer. J. Am. Chem. Soc. 112: 2910-2908.

Gomez, M., Domingo, J.L., Llobet, J.M., *et al.,* (1988) Effectiveness of Chelation Therapy with Time After Acute Vanadium Intoxication. J. Appl. Toxicol. 8: 439-444.

Grantham, JJ. (1980) The Renal Sodium Pump and Vanadate. Am.J.Physiol. 239: F97-F106.

Grantham, JJ., Glynn, IM. (1979) Renal Na, K-ATPase: Determinants of Inhibition by Vanadium. Am.J.Physiol. 236(6): F530-F535.

Gylseth, B., Leira, HL., Steinnes, E., Thomassen, Y. (1979) Vanadium in the Blood and Urine of Workers in a Feraalloy Plant. Scand. J. Work Environ.Health. 5: 188-194.

Hanauske, U., Hanauske, AR., Marshall, MH., *et al.,* (1987) Biphasic Effect of Vanadium Salts on in Vitro Tumour Colony Growth. Int. J. Cell Cloning 5: 170-178.

Heyliger, CE., Tahiliani, AG., McNeill, JH. (1985) Effect of Vanadate on Elevated Blood Glucose and Depressed Cardiac Performance of Diabetic Rats. Science. 227(4693): 1474-1477.

Hopkins, LL. Jr., Mohr, HE. (1971) The Biological Essentiality of Vanadium. In: Newer Trace Elements in Nutrition. Mertz, W., Cornatzer, WE. Ed. New York, Marcel (. Dekker, 195-213.

Hopkins, LL. Jr., Mohr, HE. (1974) Vanadium as an Essential Nutrient. Fed.Proc. 33(6): 1173-1175.

Horner, CK., Burck, D., Allison, F., Sherman, MS. (1942) Nitrogen Fixation by Azotobacter as Influenced by Molybdenum and Vanadium. J. Agric. Res. 65: 173-193.

Hudgins, PM., Bond, GH. (1979) Reversal of Vanadate Inhibition of Na,K-ATPase by Catecholamines. Res. Commun. Chem. Pathol. Pharmacol. 23(2): 313: 326.

Hudson, TOP. (1964) Vanadium: Toxicology and Biological Significance, Elsevier Publishing Company, Amsterdam.

ICRP (1960) Report of Committee II on Permissible Dose for International Radiation (1959). Recommendations of the International Commission on Radiological Protection, Oxford, Pergamon Press (ICRP Publication No. 2).

International Programme on Chemical Safety (IPCS 1988) Environmental Health Criteria: Vanadium . WHO. 81: 91-123.

Kada, T., Hirano, K., Shirasu, Y. (1980) Screening of Environmental Chemical Mutagens by the Rat-assay System with Bacillus Subtilis. Chemical Mutagens 6: 149-173.

Kalyani, P., Ramasarma, T. (1992) Polyvanadate-stimulated NADH Oxidation by the Plasma Membranes—for a Mixture of Deca and Meta Forms of Vanadate. Arch. Biochem. Biophys. 297: 244-252.

Kanematsu, N., Hara, M., Kada, T., (1980) Rat Assay and Mutagenicity Studies on Metal Compounds. Mutation Research 77: 109-116.

Lewis, CE. (1959a) The Biological Actions of Vanadium. Am. Med. Assoc. Arch. Ind. Health. 19: 419-424.

Liochev, S, Fridovich, I. (1990) Vanadate-stimulated Oxidation of NAD(P)H in the Presence of Biological Membranes and Other Sources of O_2 Arch. Biochem. Biophys. 279: 1-7.

Macara, IG. (1980) Vanadium—An Element in Search of a Role. Trends Biochem. Sci. 5: 92-94

Macara, IG., Kustin, K., Cantley, LC.Jr. (1980) Glutathione Reduces Cytoplasmic Vanadate: Mechanism and Physiology Implications. Biochim. Biophys.Acta. 629:95-106.

Maroni, M., Colombi, A., Buratti, M., Caltzaferri, G., Foa, V., Sabbioni, E., Pietra, R. (1983) Urinary Elimination of Vanadium in Boiler Cleaners. In: Proceedings of an International Conference on Heavy Metals in the Environment, London, 18-21 September, 1979, Edinburgh, CEC Consultants. 66-69.

Martin, DM., Chasteen ND. (1988) Methods in Enzymology. 158: 402-421.

Mitchell, WG., Floyd, EP. (1954) Ascorbic Acid and Ethylenediaminetetracetate (EDTA) as Antidotes in Experimental Vanadium Poisoning. Proc. Soc. Exp. Biol. Med. 85: 206-208.

Nechay, BR., Nanning, LB., Nechay, PSE., Post, RL, Branthan, JJ., Macara, IG., Kubena, LF., Philip, TD., Nielsen, FH. (1986) Role of Vanadium in Biology. Fred. Proc. 45: 123-132.

Nechay, R. (1984) Mechanism of Action of Vanadate. Ann. Rev. Pharmacol. Toxicol. 24: 501-524.

Nechay, R., Saunders, JP. (1978) Inhibition by Vanadium of Sodium and Potassium Dependent Adenosinetriphosphatase Derived from Animal and Human Tissues. J. Environ. Pathol.Toxicol. 2: 247-262.

Nielsen, FH., Ollerich, DA. (1973) Studies on a Vanadium Deficiency in Chicks. Fed. Proc. 32: 929p.

Ordhzonikidze, EK., Roschin, AV., Shalganova, IV., Bogomazov, MYA., Kazimov, MA. (1977) [On the Distribution and Elimination of Vanadium from the Organisms] Gig. Tr. Prof. Zabol. 6: 29-34 (Russian).

Orris , P., Cone, J., McQuilkin, S. (1983) Health Hazard Evaluation Report HETA 80-096-1359, Eureka Company, Bloomington, II. Washington, D.C.: U.S. Department of Health and Human Services, National Institute of Occupational Safety and Health. NTIS-PB85-163574.

Phillips, TD., Nechay, BR., Neldon. SL, Kubena, LF., Heidelbaugh, ND., Shepherd, EC., Stein, AF., Hayes, AW. (1982) Vanadium-Induced Inhibition of Renal Na^+ K^+- Adenosinetriphosphatase in the Chicken After Chronic Dietary Exposure. J. Toxicol. Environ. Health. 9: 651-661.

Priyadarshini, U., Tandon SG. (1961) Rapid Extraction and Spectrophotometric Determination of Vanadium with N-cinnamoyl-N-phenylhyrdroxylamine. Analyst. 86: 544-547.

Reznik, JB. (1954) [The Importance of Vanadium Compounds from the Point of View of Industrial Toxicology.] Vrach. Delo. 7: 627-632 (Russian).

Rifkin, RJ. (1965) *In Vitro* Inhibition of Na^+-K^+ and Mg^{2+} ATPase by Mono-, di-, and Trivalent Cations. Proc. Soc. Exp. Biol. Med. 120: 802-804.

Roitman, I., Travassas, LR., Azevedo, HP., Curry, A. (1969) Choline Trace Elements, and Aminoacids as Factors for Growth of an Enteric Yeast, Candida Slooffii. Sabouraudia J. Int. Soc. Hum. Anim. Mycol. 7: 15-19.

Roshchin, AV. (1968) [Vanadium and Its Compounds,] Moscow, Medicina Publishing House (in Russian).

Roshchin, AV., Ordzhonikidze, KE., Shalganova, IV. (1980) Vanadium - toxicity, Metabolism, Carrier State. J. Hyg. Epidemiol. Microbiol. lmmunol. 24(4): 377-383.

Schroeder, HA., Balassa, JJ., Tipton, IH. (1963). Abnormal Trace Metals in Man: Vanadium. J. Chron. Dis. 16: 1047-1071.

Schwarz, K., Milne, DB. (1971) Growth Effects of Vanadium in the Rat. Science. 174: 426-428.

Shi, X., Dalal, NS. (1993) One Electron Reduction of Vanadium (V) By Flavoenzymes/NADPH. Arch. Biochem. Biophys. 302: 300-303.

Singh, J., Nordlie, RC., Jorgenson, RA. (1980) Vanadate: A Potent Inhibitor of Multifunctional Glucose-6-phosphatase. Biochim. Biophys. Acta. 678:477-482.

Stutz, DR., Janusz, SJ. (1988) Hazardous Materials Injuries: A Handbook for Pre-hospital Care. 2nd Edition. Belsville, MD: Bradford Communications Corporation, 406-407.

Swarup, G., Cohen, S., Garters, DL. (1982) Inhibition of Membrane Phosphotyrosyl-protein Phosphatase Activity by Vanadate. Biochem. Biophys. Res. Commun. 107: 1104-1109.

Takahashi, H., Nason, A. (1957) Tungstate as a Competitive Inhibitor of Molybdate in Nitrate Assimilation and N_2 Fixation by Azotobacter. Biochim. Biophys. Acta. 23: 433-435.

Talvitie, NA., Wagner, WD. (1954) Tungstate as a Competitive Inhibitor of Molybdate in Nitrate Assimilation and N_2 Fixation by Azotobactor. Biochim. Biophys. Acta. 23: 433-435.

U.S. Department of Health, Education, and Welfare Report (1977) Occupational Exposure to Vanadium: Criteria for Recommended Standard, Washington. Nat. Instit. Occup. Safety and Health. 1-142.

Underwood, EJ. (1977) Vanadium. In: Trace Elements in Human and Animal Nutrition, 4th ed., New York, Academic Press, 388-397.

Vouk, V. (1979) Vanadium. In: Handbook on the Toxicology of Metals, Amsterdam, ed. Friberg, L, Norberg, GF., Vouk V., Amsterdam, New York, Oxford, Elsevier Science Publishers. 659-674.

Vyskocil, F., Teisinger, J., Dlouha, H. (1981) The Disparity Between Effects of Vanadate (V) and Vanadyl (IV) Ions on (Na^+K^+) ATPase and K^+-Phosphatase in Skeletal Muscle. Biochem. Biophys. Res. Commun. 100: 982-987.

Weast, RC. (1987) CRC Handbook of Chemistry and Physics, 67th ed., Boca Raton, Florida, CRC Press.

Westenfelder, C., Hamburger, RK., Garcia, ME. (1981) Effect of Vanadate on Renal Tubular Function in Rats. Am.J.Physiol. 240: F522-F529.

Zemkova, H., Teisinger, J., Vyskocil, F. (1982) The Comparison of Vanadyl (IV) and Insulin Induced Hyper-polarisation of the Mammalian Muscle Cell. Biochim.Biophys.Acta. 720: 405-410.

6

OPTIMISATION OF HARVESTING AGE OF *CATLA CATLA* IN A FRESHWATER ENVIRONMENT

Dr. Badal Das*

ABSTRACT

Catla catla is one of the most popular, culturable freshwater fish of India. Von Bertalanffy's growth equation for *Catla* has been found to be, $1_t = 1105$ $(1\text{-}e^{-0.3171(t-0.0489)}$. The annual as well as the instantaneous growth in weight decreases consistently with the advancement of age and it attains about 2 kg. body weight in two years. Total protein content of body flesh increases linearly with increase in body length and attains its optimum level corresponding to 550 mm. body length or 2 years of age. The level of fat remains almost unchanged up to certain body length and then increases exponentially. But the most rapid period of fat accumulation occurs during the second year of age. Body gets more hydrated, but loses protein and fat significantly in response to maturity. Males and females do not differ in their moisture, protein or fat profile. However spent females contain less amount of fat than their male counterpart. The calorific value of body flesh increases with increase in age but a stiff rise has been observed within 1 to 2 years of age. So, harvesting *Catla* on the completion of two years of age seems to be most judicious.

Introduction

Fish have great significance in the life of mankind, being

---

* Lecturer in Zoology, U.N. Col[illegible] of Sc. & Tech. Adaspur, Cuttack, Orissa.

an important natural source of protein and providing certain other useful products as well as economic sustenance to many nations. For developing fishery, it is necessary to understand their population dynamics, how fast they grow and reproduce the size and age at which they spawn. The growth rate in fishes is highly variable in a pond and depends upon a number of environmental factors such as temperature, amount of dissolved oxygen, ammonia, salinity, photoperiod, degree of competition, quality of food taken, age and the state of maturity. Growth of the fish is generally rapid during its initial period of life and thereafter gets retarded as it approaches asymptotic size (Natarajan & Jhingran, 1963; Ghosh, 1974 and Das & Mishra, 1990).From culture fisheries point of view, fish should be harvested sometime within its rapid period of growth so as to yield maximum fish biomass with minimum input. On the other hand, protein and fat composition of fish which determines its nutritive value to a considerable extent are also considerably influenced by a number of biological parameters such as age, growth and maturity etc.(Milroy, 1908; Johnstone, 1914; Bruce, 1924; Hickling, 1930; Tilik, 1932; Lovern & Wood, 1937; Tarr, 1959; Kukucz, 1962; Dambergs,1964; Love, 1970; and Viswanathan Nair & Rajendranathan Nair, 1985). The present discussion envisages to optimise the harvesting period of *Catla* taking into consideration both its growth rate as well as the nutritive value. For the above mentioned purpose, the moisture, protein and fat composition of body flesh have been investigated in relation to body length, age and maturity cycle. Sex related difference, impacts of spawning as well as variation in the calorific value of the body flesh have also been observed. Simultaneously the biology of fish encompassing length-weight relationship, relative condition factor, age, growth and maturity has also been investigated.

Material and Methods

Catla catla (Hamilton) belonging to family Cyprinidae were collected regularly from a nearby fish farm and their gonads were examined to ascertain the sex and maturity condition. The relative condition factor K_n was determined following Le Cren

(1951). Few scales of the region between the base of the dorsal fin and the lateral line were examined for their age determination.

Bone and scale free body flesh was taken from different regions of the body and analysed for moisture, total protein and fat composition. For this purpose, body of the fish was demarcated into the following regions :

Region I — Nape

Region II — Below the dorsal fin

Region III — Caudal peduncle

Moisture and total protein were estimated following AOAC (1960) and Micro-kjeldahl's (Hawk, 1954) method respectively. Fat was extracted by Soxhlet apparatus using petroleum spirit (60-80°c) as solvent.

To observe length and age related changes, fish with developed gonads were excluded. Maturity related changes and monthly variation in the calorific values of the body flesh were investigated only in the females belonging to 450-550mm. body length (1.5-2.5 kg).For computing calorific values, the following standard factors have been used :

Protein — 4.1 k cal./gm.

Fat — 9.1k cal./gm.

To study the impact of breeding, matured males and spent females belonging to body length 350-550mm. were investigated. It may be mentioned here that a male can undertake breeding number of times in a breeding season and thus can be considered as spent only towards the end of the season. So the term 'matured male' has been preferred over 'spent male' for the males that have been used even once for breeding.

Observations

The length-weight relationships have been found to be:-

Male – $W = 0.0000038L^{3.2115}$, $r = 0.994$

Female – $W = 0.0000029L^{3.2611}$, $r = 0.992$

Juvenile – $W = 0.0000048L^{3.1717}$, $r = 0.998$

However, test for homogeneity of their regression coefficients indicated no significant difference among them ($F = 2.8$, $n_1 = 2$, $n_2 = 405$).Thus a common regression equation was found out which is applicable for male, female and juvenile:

$$W = 0.0000044L^{3.1902}$$

Comparison of exponent of this equation with that of the isometric growth, *i.e.*, 3.0, indicated a significant difference between them ($t = 35.5$, $n = 411$).The relative condition factor K_n has been found to be 1.01, 1.04 and 1.0 respectively for juvenile, male and female. The Von Bertalanffy's growth parameters have been determined to be:

$$1_t = 1105\ (1\text{-}e^{-0.3171(t.0.0489)})$$

Using the above derived growth parameters; length at ages has been calculated (*Table-6.1*) and the emperical growth curve has also been drawn (*Fig. 6.1*).The length age data were used to estimate fish weight at different ages, annual growth in weight as well as the instantaneous rate of growth (*Table-6.2*).The gonado-somatic index was remarkably high during June to August with peak in July (*Fig. 6.2*).

Table 6.1 Length at ages derived from scale study and Von Bertalanffy's growth equation

Age in years	*No. of rings in the scale*	*Length at capture (m.m.)*	*Calculated length derived from scale study (mm.)*	*Calculated length using V.B.G. equation (m.m.)*	*Annual growth in length %*
1				288	
					77
2	1	527	509	509	
					32
3	2	698	670	671	
					18
4	3	828	791	789	
					11
5	4	915	875	875	

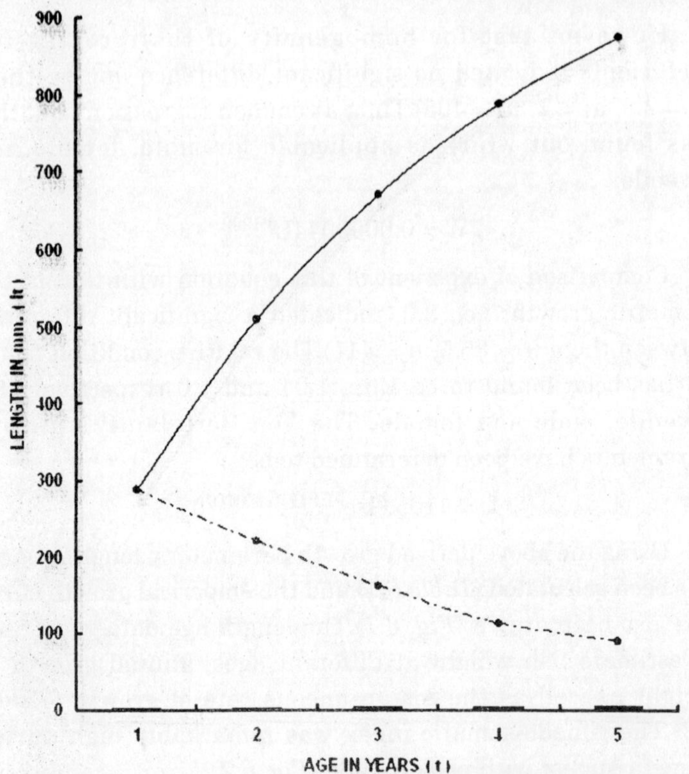

Fig. 6.1 The emperical growth curve of *Catla catla*.

Table 6.2 Annual and Instantaneous Rate of Growth in Weight

Age in years	*No. of rings in the scale*	*Average weight (gm.)*	*Annual growth in weight*	*Instantaneous length rate of growth*
1	Nil	300		
			570	1.9021
2	1	2012		
			150	0.9143
3	2	5020		
			80	0.5881
4	3	9039		
			36	0.3135
5	4	12368		

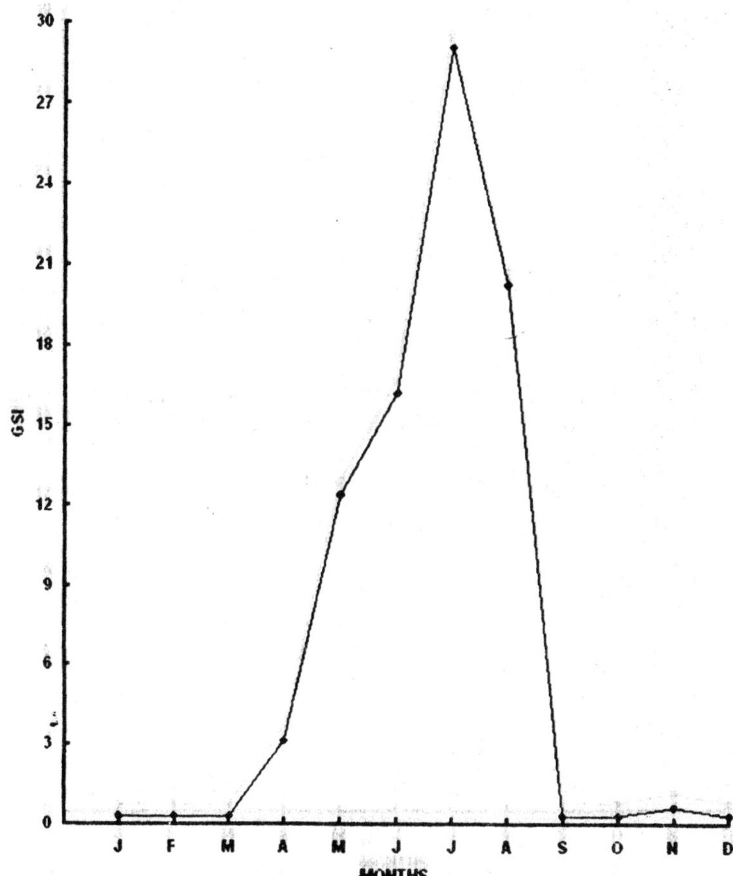

Fig. 6.2 Monthly variation in the gonado-somatic index of *Catla catla*.

Moisture composition of *Region-I, II,* and *III* remained almost unchanged up to 300,325 and 400mm. body length in male and 325,375 and 400mm. in the female respectively (*Fig. 6.3a*). However, the level of moisture declined linearly with further increase in body length. Comparison of regression coefficients of the three regions of male ($F = 0.5$, $n_1 = 2$, $n_2 = 92$) as well as of the female ($F = 1.88$, $n_1 = 2$, $n_2 = 74$) indicated no significant difference. For the comparison of moisture profile of male and female, their body length-moisture content regression equations were tested for equality. Such test indicated no significant difference between them (*Table 6.3*). So far the impact of age is concerned, reduction in the moisture composition was marginal up to one year of age. But thereafter it reduced sharply baring in the *Region-III* where the reduction was comparatively less (*Fig. 6.4(a)*). Body got increasingly hydrated with the advancement of maturity condition (*Fig. 6.5(a)*). However; a rapid phase of hydration has been observed beyond G.S.I-4.5 in case of *Region I and II* and beyond G.S.I-6.0 in the *Region III*. Moisture composition of *Region I* and *II* of the spent female was significantly higher than their counterparts of matured male (*Table 6.4(a)*).

Table 6.3 Tests for the equality of regression equations for body length-moisture content relationhsips of male and female
A—Region I, B—Region II, C—Region III.

A—Region I

Source of variation	*df*	*SS*	*MS*	$F = \frac{MSH_0}{MSE}$
Due to H_0	2 2(p–1)	8.01 SSH_0 (S_2^2–S_1^2)	4.005 MSH_0	0.82
Residual (Separate regressions)	63 (n-2p)	304.46 SSE (S_1^2)	4.832 MSE	
Residual under H_0 (Common regression)	65 (n-2)	312.47 S_2^2		

B—Region II

Source of variation	*df*	*SS*	*MS*	$F = \frac{MSH_0}{MSE}$
Due to H_0	2 2(p–1)	15.38 SSH_0 (S_2^2–S_1^2)	7.69 MSH_0	1.32
Residual (Separate regressions)	57 (n-2p)	330.03 SSE (S_1^2)	5.79 MSE	
Residual under H_0 (Common regression)	59 (n-2)	345.41 S_2^2		

(*Contd.*)

C—Region III

Source of variation	*df*	*SS*	*MS*	$F = \dfrac{MSH_0}{MSE}$
Due to H_0	2 2(p–1)	1.5 $SSH_0\ (S_2^2–S_1^2)$	0.75 MSH_0	
				0.46
Residual (Separate regressions)	46 (n-2p)	73.66 SSE (S_1^2)	1.60 MSE	
Residual under H_0 (Common regression)	48 (n-2)	75.16 S_2^2		

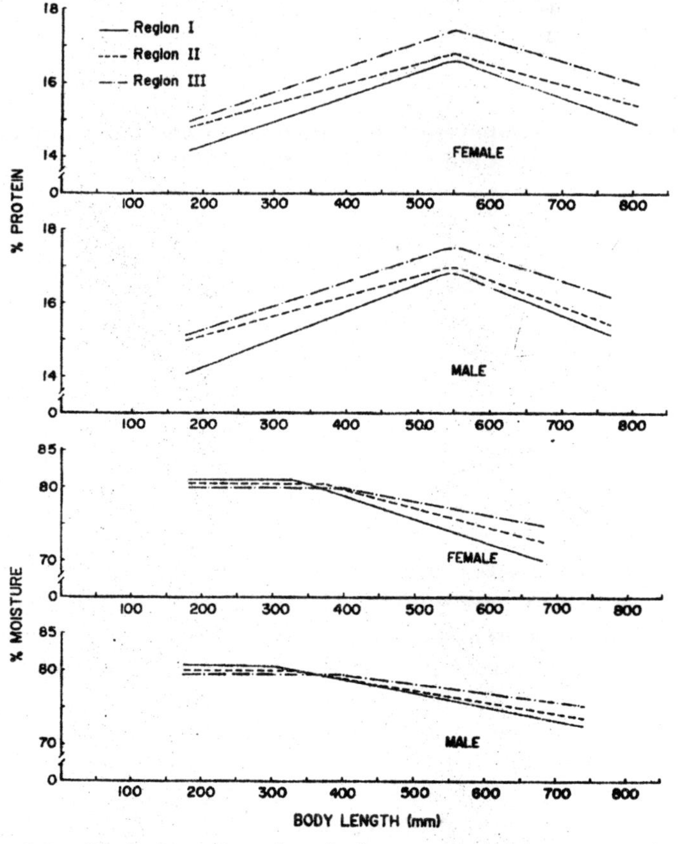

Fig. 6.3 Body length related changes in the moisture and protein composition of *Catla catla*.

Table 6.4(*a*) Comparison of moisture content of matured male and spent female *Catla catla* by 't' test.

Body length (mm.)	*No. of obs.*	*Region*	*I*		*II*		*III*	
		Sex	Male	Female	Male	Female	Male	Female
		Mean % of Moisture ±	78.41	80.92	78.39	80.77	78.48	79.8
350-550	31	SD	3.27	2.12	3.57	2.04	2.17	1.31
		Calculated "t"	2.372*		2.259*		2.037	
		% of difference	3.2		3.0			

*Significant at 5% (P<0.05).

Table 6.4(*b*) Comparison of fat content of matured male and spent female *Catla catla* by 't' test.

Body length (mm.)	*No. of obs.*	*Region*	*I*		*II*		*III*	
		Sex	Male	Female	Male	Female	Male	Female
		Mean % of Fat ±	2.66	1.01	2.51	0.82	1.5	0.59
350-550	25	SD	1.84	0.92	2.28	0.76	1.1	0.29
		Calculated "t"	2.93*		2.71*		3.29*	
% of difference			163.4		206.09		154.2	

In both the sexes, protein content increased linearly with increase in body length up to 550 mm. but declined thereafter with further increase in body length (*Fig 6.3(b)*). Test for homogeneity of regression coefficients of three regions of male (F = 0.56, $n_1 = 2$, $n_2 = 180$) as well as of female (F = 0.3, $n_1 = 2$, $n_2 = 118$) indicated no significant difference among them. Test for equality of body length-protein content regression equations of both the sexes did not indicate any sex related significant difference (*Table-6.5*). Protein composition of the flesh increased with increase in age and reached its peak on second year of age (*Fig. 6.4(b)*).The level of protein also declined in response to advancement of maturity condition However, a sharp decline has been observed within G.S.I. about 12.5-21.0 (*Fig. 6.5(b)*).

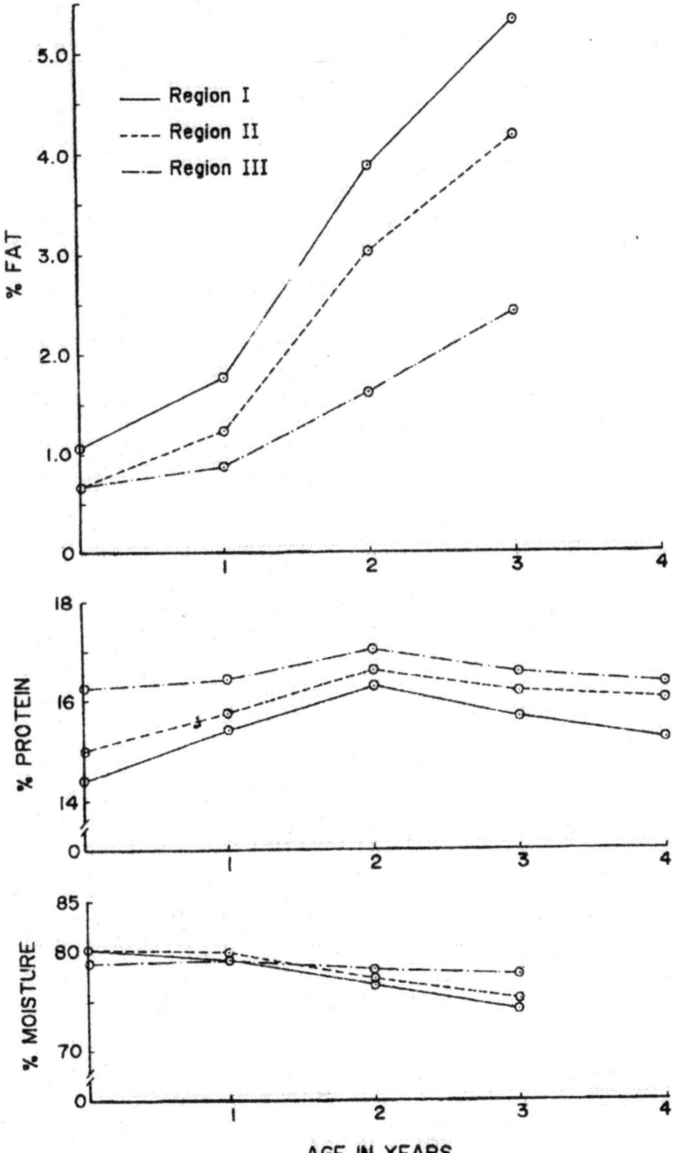

Fig. 6.4 Age related changes in the moisture, protein and fat composition of *Catla catla*.

Table 6.5 **Tests for the equality of regression equations for body length-protein content relationships of male and female. A—Region I, B—Region II, C—Region III.**

A—Region I

Source of variation	*df*	*SS*	*MS*	$F = \frac{MSH_0}{MSE}$
Due to H_0	2 2(p–1)	0.34 SSH_0 (S_2^2–S_1^2)	0.17 MSH_0	0.11
Residual (Separate regressions)	103 (n-2p)	158.62 SSE (S_1^2)	1.54 MSE	
Residual under H_0 (Common regression)	105 (n-2)	158.96 S_2^2		

B—Region II

Source of variation	*df*	*SS*	*MS*	$F = \frac{MSH_0}{MSE}$
Due to H_0	2 2(p–1)	2.15 SSH_0 (S_2^2–S_1^2)	1.075 MSH_0	0.75
Residual (Separate regressions)	101 (n-2p)	144.54 SSE (S_1^2)	1.431 MSE	
Residual under H_0 (Common regression)	103 (n-2)	146.69 S_2^2		

C—Region III

Source of variation	*df*	*SS*	*MS*	$F = \frac{MSH_0}{MSE}$
Due to H_0	2 2(p–1)	2.95 SSH_0 (S_2^2–S_1^2)	1.475 MSH_0	1.04
Residual (Separate regressions)	94 (n-2p)	132.34 SSE (S_1^2)	1.407 MSE	
Residual under H_0 (Common regression)	96 (n-2)	135.29 S_2^2		

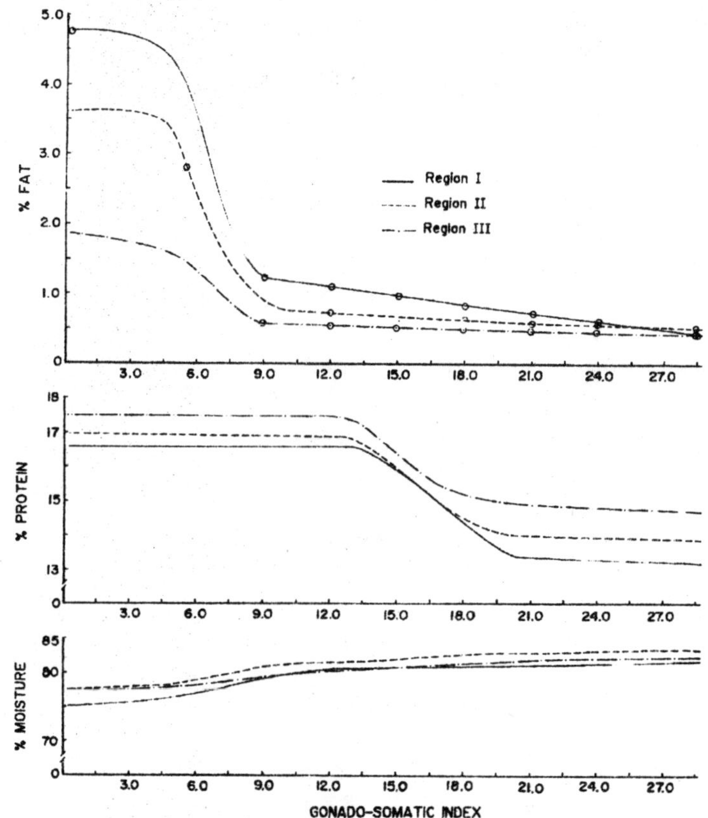

Fig. 6.5 Maturity related changes in the moisture, protein and fat composition of *Catla catla*.

In both the sexes the fat content of *Region I, II,* and *III* remained almost unchanged up to about 350, 400 and 450 mm. body length respectively but thereafter increased exponentially (*Fig. 6.6*). To compare the rate of increase of fat composition in the different regions of the body, the exponential equations were transformed to linear form and their regression coefficients were compared. Such tests did not indicate any significant difference in the males ($F = 0.71$, $n_1 = 2$, $n_2 = 57$) as well as in the females ($F = 0.87$, $n_1 = 2$, $n_2 = 71$). Test for equality of body length-fat content relationship of male and female did not indicate any significant difference (*Table-6.6*).The level of fat

Table 6.6 **Tests for the equality of exponential equations for body length-fat content relationships of male and female. A—Region I, B—Region II, C—Region III.**

A—Region I

Source of variation	*df*	*SS*	*MS*	$F = \frac{MSH_0}{MSE}$
Due to H_0	2 2(p–1)	0.0961 SSH_0 (S_2^2–S_1^2)	0.0480 MSH_0	
				0.88
Residual (Separate regressions)	46 (n-2p)	2.5108 SSE (S_1^2)	0.0545 MSE	
Residual under H_0 (Common regression)	48 (n-2)	2.6069 S_2^2		

B—Region II

Source of variation	*df*	*SS*	*MS*	$F = \frac{MSH_0}{MSE}$
Due to H_0	2 2(p–1)	0.0652 SSH_0 (S_2^2–S_1^2)	0.0326 MSH_0	
				0.376
Residual (Separate regressions)	46 (n-2p)	3.9856 SSE (S_1^2)	0.0866 MSE	
Residual under H_0 (Common regression)	48 (n-2)	4.0508 S_2^2		

C—Region III

Source of variation	*df*	*SS*	*MS*	$F = \frac{MSH_0}{MSE}$
Due to H_0	2 2(p–1)	0.0465 SSH_0 (S_2^2–S_1^2)	0.02325 MSH_0	
				0.773
Residual (Separate regressions)	36 (n-2p)	1.0826 SSE (S_1^2)	0.03007 MSE	
Residual under H_0 (Common regression)	38 (n-2)	1.1291 S_2^2		

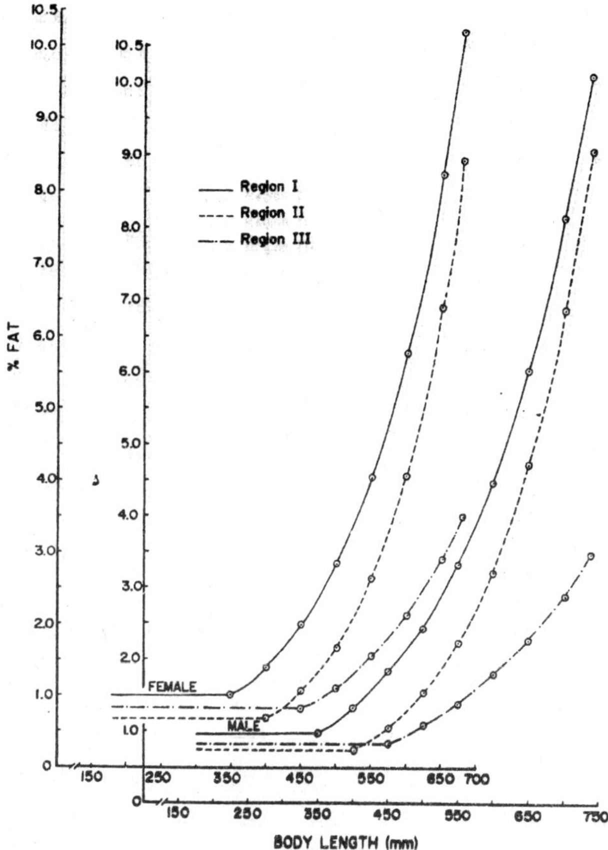

Fig. 6.6 Body length related changes in the fat composition of *Catla catla*

continued to increase with increase in age but a rapid phase of increase has been observed within 1 to 2 years of age (*Fig 6.4(c)*). However, the fat composition indicated continuous decline with the advancement of maturity condition. But a sharp decline has been observed within G.S.I.-4.25 to 9.0 (*Fig. 6.5(c)*). Spent females have been observed to contain significantly less amount of fat than their male counterpart (*Table-6.4(b)*).

The details of relationships of body length with moisture, protein and fat composition in both the sexes have been provided in the *Table-6.7*.

Table 6.7 Body length—moisture, protein and fat relationships in male and female *Catla catla*

Sex	*Body length range (mm.)*	*Region*	*No. of obs.*	*Body length-moisture content relationship*	*"r"*	*P.E. ±*	*S.E.E. ±*
Male	330-737	I	40	y = 85.5–0.0170x	–0.749*	0.046	1.506
	325-737	II	33	y = 86.0-0.0164x	–0.665*	0.065	2.139
	400-737	III	25	y=82.9–0.0097x	–0.447*	0.107	1.067
Female	325-680	I	27	y=92.1-0.0324x	–0.689*	0.068	2.497
	375-680	II	28	y=87.2-0.0207x	–0.545*	0.089	2.691
	400-680	III	25	y=85.7-0.0153x	–0.627*	0.081	1.377

x = Body length, *y* = %of moisture content. *Significant at 5% (P < 0.05)

Sex	*Body length range (mm.)*	*Region*	*No. of obs.*	*Body length-protein content relationship*	*"r"*	*P.E. ±*	*S.E.E. ±*
Male	175-550	I	64	y=12.7839+0.0074x	–0.59*	0.054	1.28
	175-550	II	63	y=13.992+0.0056x	–0.53*	0.006	1.15
	175-550	III	59	y=14.1224+0.0061x	–0.53*	0.062	1.20
Female	180-550	I	43	y=12.9637+0.0067x	0.62*	0.063	1.27
	180-550	II	42	y=13.8208+0.0053x	0.52*	0.075	1.25
	180-550	III	39	y=13.9946+0.0059x	0.55*	0.074	1.15

x = Body length, *y* = % of protein content. *Significant at 5% (P < 0.05)

Sex	*Body length range (mm.)*	*Region*	*No. of obs.*	*Body length-fat content relationship*	*"r"*	*P.E. ±*	*S.E.E. ±*
Male	350-737	I	25	y=0.120x1.006046x	0.771*	0.054	
	400-737	II	22	y=0.035x1.007572x	0.696*	0.074	
	450-737	III	16	y=0.089x1.004985x	0.747*	0.074	
Female	350-680	I	25	y=0.082x1.007125x	0.720*	0.064	
	400-680	II	28	y=0.018x1.009085x	0.735*	0.058	
	450-680	III	24	y=0.[illegible]1.006269x	0.745*	0.061	

x = Body length, *y* = % of fat content. *Significant at 5% (P < 0.05

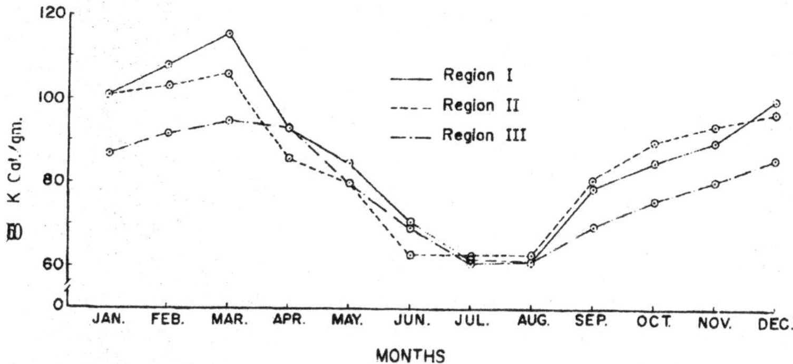

Fig. 6.7 Monthly variation in the calorific value of *Catla catla*

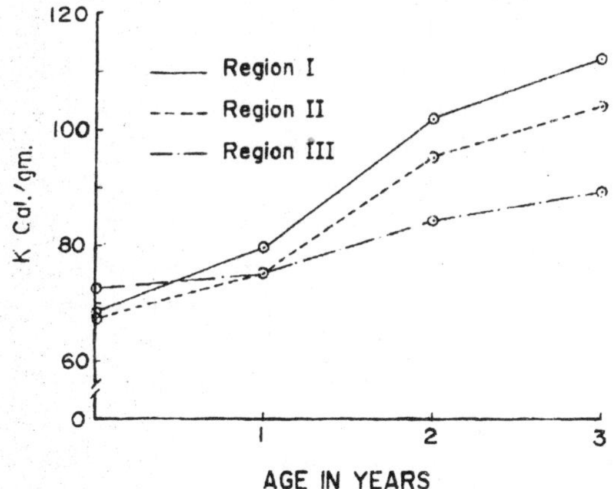

Fig. 6.8 Age related changes in the calorific value of *Catla catla*

The calorific value of body flesh started receding after March and reached its lowest level during June to August (*Fig. 6.7*). So far age related changes in the calorific value is concerned, the latter increased with age but a stiff rise was observed within 1 to 2 years of age (*Fig. 6.8*).

Discussion

Length-weight relationship has been observed to measure any variation from the expected weight of individual fish as an indication of fatness or general well-being. The detailed investigation has not recorded any statistically significant difference among the exponents of length-weight relationships of juvenile, male and female. Natarajan and Jhingran (1963),

Rita Kumari and Balakrishnan Nair (1978) and Vinci and Sugunan (1981) also reported similar phenomenon in different groups of fish. However significant departure of exponent of length-weight relationship of *Catla* from that of in the isometric growth may be attributed to the peculiar shape of its body. In *Catla* body is deep and the depth is 3.0 to 3.5 in total length (Day, 1878).The K_n values for juvenile, male and female have been found to be either 1.0 or slightly higher, which indicates that the fish samples used in the investigation were in good condition. According to Love (1970) fish grow continuously as long as they live, though in a slow pace after certain phase of rapid growth. Information on the growth rate of a fish is essential for determining its optimum harvesting size. The experimental observation reveals that *Catla* attains 288, 509, 671, 789 and 875mm. body length on the 1st, 2nd, 3rd, 4th and 5th year of age. Thus the annual increment in length is 288, 221, 162, 113 and 91mm in the 1st, 2nd, 3rd, 4th and 5th year respectively (*Fig. 6.1*).The annual growth in weight and instantaneous rate of growth also indicated a consistent decreasing tendency (*Table-6.2*). All these facts concurrently indicate that the rate of growth of *Catla* is highest in its first year of life and diminishes continuously thereafter till the asymptotic size is reached. In the first year of life the fish consumes less amount of food as they are smaller in size but their capacity to convert food to flesh is very high. Whereas in the older fish, the food requirement increases as they grow in size but their growth rate is reduced as their capacity to convert food to body biomass is decreased. This fact seems to have great relevance to culture fisheries as supplementary feeding accounts for about 60 per cent of the expenditure. Though the rate of growth is highest in the first year of life, harvesting at this age may not be profitable as they do not reach suitable marketable size at this age. However, in the second year of age, even though the rate of growth is comparatively low, the fish attains about 2 kg body weights which is considered as suitable marketable size. In the subsequent years of age, the fish no doubt attains larger size but the rate of growth is diminished further. Taking these facts into consideration it seems most judicious to harvest *Catla* on the completion of two years of age.

It is evident from the body length-moisture content relationships, that decline in the level of moisture is initiated first in the *Region I* and then followed by in the *Region II* and *III* in a sequence. This phase wise initiation of reduction in the moisture content is a reflection of sequential accumulation of fat in the body. It may be mentioned here that there exists an inverse relationship between the moisture and fat composition of fish tissue (Brandes and Dietrich, 1958; Jafri, 1973; Selvaraj, 1984; Salam, A. and M. Y. Janjua, 1992; M. Ali *et.al.,* 2004).The absence of any significant difference among the slopes of body length-moisture content regression equations of different regions of the body in either sex, suggests that the level of moisture declines at equal rate in all the regions of the body. So far age is concerned; remarkable decline has been observed beyond one year of age. Variation in the level of moisture is known to be linked with the reproductive cycle(Love,1960; and Pandey *et.al.,* 1976).The present data also indicates that the body gets increasingly hydrated with the advancement of gonadial maturity and thus the body remains in a highly hydrated condition during the breeding season, *i.e.;* June to August.

Protein composition in both the sexes reaches its optimum level corresponding to 550mm.body length. The increase is to the extent of about 18 per cent, 14 per cent and 16 per cent in the *Region-I, II,* and *III* respectively. However the rate of increase seems to be equal as no significant difference has been observed among the regression coefficients of body length-protein content relationships. So far age is concerned, the peak value of protein has been observed on the second year of age. That the protein content of fish is dependent on its maturity condition and season has been highlighted by Lovern and Wood(1937), McBride *et.al.,* (1959), Dambergs (1964) and Gras et al(1967 a). In *Catla,* protein content is affected when the GSI exceeds 13.0 and assumes its lowest level in the ripe fish, *i.e.,* during June to August. The reduction is to the extent of 19 per cent, 18 per cent and 16 per cent in the *Region I, II,* and *III* respectively. Sharp decline in the level of protein corresponding to GSI 13.0 to 20.0 may be due to massive protein mobilisation during the phase of maturity.

The experimental observations also indicate that the fat composition remains almost unchanged up to a certain body length and thereafter increases exponentially. Such increase in both the sexes is initiated in a sequential manner from the *Region I* to *III*, suggesting that accumulation of fat starts from behind the head and proceeds towards the caudal end. However, the absence of any significant difference among the regression coefficients of body length-fat content relationships indicates that the increase in the level of fat occurs at equal rate in all the three regions of the body. But the most rapid period of fat accumulation has been observed to be the 2nd year of age. There is a considerable body of literature on the variation of fat composition of fish flesh in relation to sexual maturity (Clark and Almy, 1918; Johnstone, 1918; McBride, 1959; Idler and Bitners, 1960 and Ramachandran Nair and Gopakumar, 1981). Fat content of *Catla* has been observed to decline consistently with increase in maturity condition and thus reaches its lowest level in the ripe fish, *i.e.,* during June to August. The depletion of fat is to the extent of 92 per cent, 83 per cent and 76 per cent in the *Region I, II,* and *III* respectively. It is evident from the detailed investigation that depletion of fat precedes protein depletion in response to maturity. Spent females have been observed to contain remarkably less amount of fat than their male counterpart as the spawning stress is more severe in the former. However, no other significant sex related difference has been observed in the level of moisture, protein or fat. Monthly variation in the calorific value well matches with the maturity cycle of the fish and reaches its maximum level during February to March. So far age is concerned, the calorific value increases with increase in age but a stiff increase has been observed within 1 to 2 years of age.

All these facts concurrently indicate that harvesting *Catla* just on the completion of 2 years of age will be most judicious.

References

1. A.O.A.C. (1960). Official Methods of Analysis, 9th Edition. Association of Official Agricultural Chemists, Washington.
2. Brandes, C.H. and Dietrich, R. 1958. Observations on the Correlations Between Fat and Water Content and the Fat

Distribution in Commonly Eaten Fish. Verroff. Inst. Meeresforsch. Bremerh. 5: 299-305.

3. Bruce, J.R.I. 1924. Changes in the Chemical Composition of the Tissues of the Herring in Relation to Age and Maturity. Biochem. J. 18: 469-485.
4. Clark, E. D. and Almy, L. H. 1918. A Chemical Study of Food Fishes. J. Biol. Chem. 33: 483 - 490.
5. Dambergs, N. 1964. Extractives of Fish Muscle. 4. Seasonal Variations of Fat, Water-soluble, Protein and Water in Cod *(Gadus morhua* L.) Fillets. J. Fish. Res. Bd. Canada, 21:703-709.
6. Das, M. and Mishra, B. 1990. Studies on Certain Aspects of Nutritive Value of Indian Halibut, *Psettodes Erumei* with Special Reference to Its Body Asymmetry. Fish. Technol, 27: 103-108.
7. Day, F. 1878. The Fishes of India, William Dawson and Sons Ltd., London, (Reproduced in 1958).
8. Ghosh, K. K. 1974. On the Choice of a Growth Curve for Indian Major Carps, Von Bertalanffy or Gompertz? J. Ind. Soc. Agr, New Delhi 26(2):57-70.
9. Gras, J., Reynaud, R., Gamoty, L., Frey, J. and Henry, J.C. 1967 a. Biochemical Study of Fishes. 1. Six-monthly Variations in the Water and Protein Content of the Muscle Tissue of Rainbow Trout *(Salmo gairdnerii* Rich). Experientia, 23: 430-431.
10. Hickling, C.F. 1930.The Natural History of the Hake. Fishery Invest. London. Ser. 2, 12(1); 78.
11. Idler, D.R. and Bitners, I. 1960. Biochemical Studies on Sockeye Salmon During Spawning Migration. IX.Fat, Protein and Water in the Major Internal Organs and Cholesterol in the Liver and Gonads of the Standard Fish.J.Fish.Res.Bd.Canada. 17:113-122.
12. Jafri, A.K. 1973. Fat and Water Distribution Patterns in the Flesh of the Common Catfish, *Wallago Attu* (Bl. & Schn.) Fish.Technol, 10 (2): 138-141.
13. Johnstone, J.1914.Ann.Rep.Lancashire Sea Fish.Lab, 23: 154-161.
14. Johnstone.J. 1918. The Value of the Herring as Food. Nature, London, 102: 6-7.
15. Kukucz, J.T. 1962. Effects of Biological Factors (Sex, Seasonal Races, Spawning Migrations) on Fat, Protein and Water, Their

Distribution in-Sea-trout. In, Fish in Nutrition, Edited by E.Heen and R. Kreuzer. Fishing News (Books) Ltd., England., p. 447.

16. Le Cren, E.D. 1951. The Length-weight Relationship and Seasonal Cycle in Gonad Weight and Condition in the Perch *(Perca fluviatilis).* J. Anim. Ecol, 20 (2): 201-219.

17. Love, R.M. 1960. Water Content of Cod *(Gadus Callarias* L.) Muscle.Nature, London, 185:692.

18. Love, R.M. 1970. The Chemical Biology of Fishes. Academic Press, London and New York.

19. Lovern, J.A. and Wood, H. 1937. Variations in the Chemical Composition of the Herrings.J.Mar.Biol.Ass.U.K, 22: 281-293.

20. M, Ali, Salam, A. Goher, S. Tassaduqe, K. and Latif, M. 2004. Studies on Fillet Composition of Fresh Water Farmed *Labeo Rohita* in Relation to Body Size, Collected from Government Fish Seed Hatchery, Mian Channu Pakistan. Journal of Biological Sciences, 4 (1): 40-46,

21. McBride, J.R., MacLeod, R.A. and Idler, D.R. 1959. Proximate Analysis of Pacific Herring *(Clupea Pallasii)* and Evaluation of Tester's "Fat Factor".J.Fish.Res.Bd.Canada, 16 (5): 679-684.

22. Milroy, T.H. 1908. Changes in the Chemical Composition of the Herring During the Reproductive Period. Biochem. J., 3: 366-389.

23. Natarajan, A.V. and Jhingran, A.G. 1963. On the Biology of *Catla catla* (Ham.) from the River Yamuna. Proc. Nat. Inst. Sci. India (B), 29(3): 326 -355.

24. Oser, B.L. 1971. Hawk's Physiological Chemistry.Tata McGraw-Hill Publishing Company Ltd., New Delhi.

25. Pandey, B.N., Datta Munshi, J.S., Choubey, B.J.and Pandey, P.K. 1976. Seasonal Variation in Body Composition in Relation to Breeding Cycle Off an Air-breathing Fish, *Heteropneustes Fossilis* (Bloch.) J. Inland Fish.Soc.India, 8: 91-96.

26. Ramachandran Nair, K.G. and Gopakumar, K. 1981. Influence of Sex, Spawning, Starvation and Water Temperature on Fatty Acid Composition in *Tilapia Mossambica.Fish.Technol,* 18: 123-127.

27. Rita Kumari, S.D. and Balakrishnan Nair, N. 1978. Length-weight Relationship of the Loaches *Noemacheilus Triangularis*

(Day) and *Lepidocephalus Thermalis* (Cuv. & Val.). Matsya, 4: 52-58.

28. Salam, A. and M. Y. Janjua, 1992. The Relationship Between Changes in Body Size, Condition Factor and Body Composition in Young Rohu, *Labeo Rohita*. J. Res. (Sci), B.Z. University, Pakistan, 4: 7-13.

29. Selvaraj, G.S.D. 1984. A Note on the Biochemical Composition of the Indian Shad, *Ilisha Melastoma* (Schneidev). Indian J. Fish., 31(1) : 161-165.

30. Tarr, H.L.A. 1959. Biochemical Changes in Fish During Maturation. Proc. 20th Ann. Biol. Colloquium. Oregon State College, April, 1959.

31. Tilik, Z.E. 1932. Changes in the Chemical Composition of the Flesh of the Svir Salmon in Relation to Spawning Migration. Izv. Vses. Inst. Ozern. Rechn. Ryb, 14; 133-148.

32. Vinci, G.K. and Sugunan, V.V. 1981. Biology of *Labeo Calbasu* (Hamilton) of Nagarjunasagar Reservoir, A.P., India. J.Inland Fish. Soc. India, 13 (2): 22-39.

33. Viswanathan Nair, P.G. and Rajendranathan Nair, M. 1985. Fatty Acid Composition of Muscle and Skin Lipids of Oil Sardine. In, Harvest and Post Harvest Technology of Fish, a Volume Based on the Symposium on Harvest and Post Harvest Technology of Fish Sponsored by the Society of Fisheries Technologists (India) During 24-27 Nov. 1982. Published by Society of Fisheries Technologists (India) p. 744.

7

STEM CELL TECHNOLOGY AND IT'S FUTURE

Rajeev Basumatary *
Manuj Kr. Bharali **
*Ramesh Ch. Kataria****

Introduction

Stem cells have two important characteristics that distinguish them from other types of cells. First, they are unspecialised cells that renew themselves for long periods through cell division. The second is that under certain physiologic or experimental conditions, they can be induced to become cells with special functions such as the beating cells of the heart muscle or the insulin-producing cells of the pancreas. Stem cells in humans and animals are primal undifferentiated cells that retain the ability to divide and differentiate into other cell types. In higher plants this function is the defining property of the meristematic cells. Stem cells have the ability to act as a repair system for the body, because they can divide and differentiate, replenishing other cells as long as the host organism is alive.

Stem cells are cells that have the remarkable potential to develop into many different cell types in the body. Serving as sort of repair system for the body, they can theoretically divide without limit to replenish other cells for as long as the person or animal is still alive. When a stem cell divides, each "daughter" cell has the potential to either refrain a stem cell or become another type of cell with a more specialised function, such as a muscle cell, a red blood cell, or a brain cell.

* D.R. College, Golaghat, Assam.
** Rajiv Gandhi University, Itanagar, Arunachal Pradesh.
*** Post Graduate College, Mandi, Himachal Pradesh.

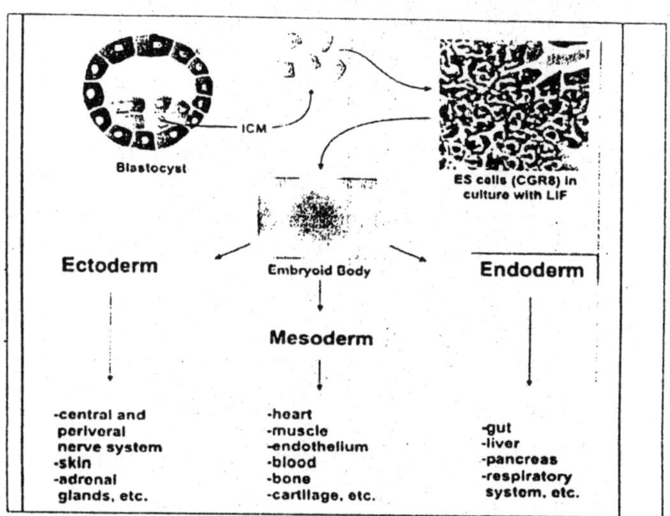

Fig. 7.1 Formation of Body Parts from Embryo

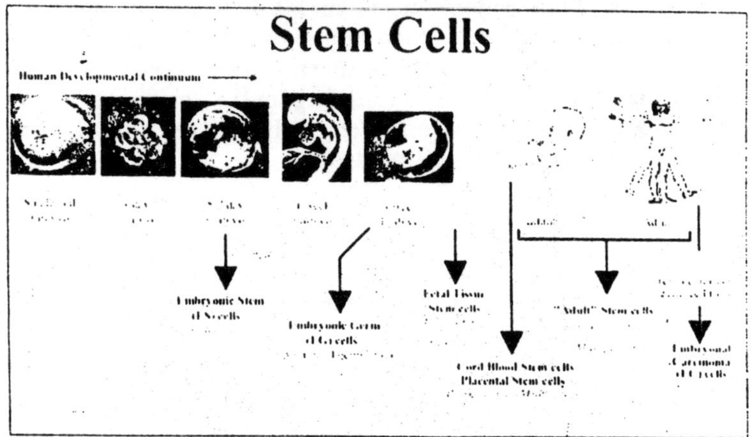

Fig. 7.2 Source and Nature of Stem Cells

The Unique Properties of All Stem Cells

Stem cells differ from other kinds of cells in the body. All stem cells—regardless of their source—have three general properties: they are capable of dividing and renewing themselves for long periods; they are unspecialised; and they can give rise to specialised cell types.

Stem Cells are Unspecialised

One of the fundamental properties of a stem cell is that it does not have any tissue-specific structures that allow it to perform specialised functions. A stem cell cannot work with its neighbours to pump blood through the body (like a heart muscle cell); it cannot carry molecules of oxygen through the bloodstream (like a red blood cell); and it cannot fire electrochemical signals to other cells that allow the body to move or speak (like a nerve cell). However, unspecialised stem celis can give rise to specialised cells, including heart muscle cells, blood cells, or nerve cells.

Stem Cells are Capable of Dividing and Renewing Themselves for Long Periods

Unlike muscle cells, blood cells, or nerve cells—which do not normally replicate themselves—stem cells may replicate many times. When cells replicate themselves many times over it is called proliferation. A starting population of stem cells that proliferates for many months in the laboratory can yield millions of cells. If the resulting cells continue to be unspecialised, like the parent stem cells, the cells are said to be capable of long-term self-renewal.

Stem Cell Types

Stem cells are categorised by both *potency* and *source.*

A. Potency

Stem cell potency specifies the ameliorative potential of the cell type and accordingly there are three types of stem cells:

Totipotent stem cells are produced from the fusion of an egg and sperm cell. Cells produced by the first few divisions of the fertilised egg cell are also totipotent. These cells can grow into any type of cell without exception;

Pluripotent stem cells are the descendants of totipotent cells and can grow into any cell type except for totipotent stem cells;

Multipotent stem cells can produce only cells of a closely related family of cells (*e.g.* blood cells such as red blood cells, white blood cells and platelets).

Unipotent cells can produce only one cell type, but have the property of self-renewal which distinguishes them from non-stem cells.

B. Sources

Stem cells are also categorised according to their source, as either adult, embryonic and cord blood stem cells.

Adult stem cells are undifferentiated cells found among differentiated cells of a specific tissue and are mostly multipotent cells. They are more accurately called *somatic* stem cells, because they need not come from adults but can also come from children or umbilical cords. Particularly interesting are adult stem cells termed "spore-like cells". They arc present in all tissues and seem to survive long time periods and harsh conditions.

Embryonic stem cells are cultured cells obtained from the undifferentiated inner mass cells of an early stage human embryo (sometimes called a blastocyst, which is an embryo that is between 50 to 150 cells). Embryonic stem cell research is "thought to have much greater developmental potential than adult stem cells," according to the National Institutes of Health. Research using embryonic stem cells remains at the zenith of stem cell science because, unlike somatic cells, embryonic stem cells are totipotent. However, research using stem cells derived from the'human embryo is still in the basic research phase, as these stem cells were first isolated in 1998 (at least for humans), whereas adult stem cells have been studied since the 1960s. Research with embryonic stem cells derived from humans is controversial because, in order to start a stem cell 'line' or lineage, the destruction of a human embryo and/or therapeutic cloning is usually required. Some believe this to be a slippery slope to reproductive cloning and tantamount to the objectification of a potential human being. In an attempt to overcome these moral, political and ethical hurdles, medical researchers have been experimenting with alternative techniques of obtaining embryonic stem cells by extraction, which does not involve cloning and/or the destruction of a human embryo.

Cord blood stem cells are derived from the blood of the placenta and umbilical cord after birth. Since 1988 these cord blood stem cells have been used to treat Gunther's disease, Hunter syndrome, Hurler syndrome, Acute lymphocytic leukemia and many more problems occurring mostly in children. Umbilical cord blood use has become so common that there are now umbilical cord blood banks that accept donations from parents. It is collected by removing the umbilical cord, cleansing it and withdrawing blood from the umbilical vein. This blood is then immediately analysed for infectious agents and the tissue-type is determined. The cord blood is processed and depleted of red blood cells before being stored in liquid nitrogen for later use, at which point it is thawed, washed of the cryoprotectant, and injected through a vein of the patient. This kind of treatment, where the stem cells are collected from another donor, is called *allogeneic* treatment. When the cells are collected from the same patient on whom they will be used, it is called *autologous* and when collected from identical individuals (*i.e.* nomozygous twin), it is referred to as syngeneic.

Research on stem cells is advancing knowledge about how an organism develops from a single cell and how healthy cells replace damaged cells in adult organisms. This promising area of science is also leading scientists to investigate the possibility of cell-based therapies to treat disease, which is often referred to as regenerative or reparative medicine.

Pluripotent stem cells are isolated from human embryos that are a few days old. Cells from these embryos can be used to create pluripotent stem cell "lines"—cell cultures that can be grown indefinitely in the laboratory. Pluripotent stem cell lines have also been developed from fetal tissue obtained from fetal tissue (older than 8 weeks of development).

Once a stem cell line is established from a cell in the body, it is essentially immortal, no matter how it was derived. That is, the researcher using the line will not have to go through the rigorous procedure necessary to isolate stem cells again. Once established, a cell line can be grown in the laboratory indefinitely and cells may be frozen for storage or distribution to other researchers.

Sources of Stem Cells

The main clinical application of stem cells is as a source of donor cells to be used to replace cells in transplantation therapy. Stem cells can be obtained from several sources:

- *Spare embryos:* stem cells can come from leftover embryos stored at fertility clinics that were not used by couples to have children.
- *Special purpose embryos:* embryos are created in vitro fertilisation (artificially in the lab) for the sole purpose of extracting their stem cells.
- *Cloned embryos:* embryos are cloned in labs using somatic nuclear transfer method in order to harvest their stem cells.
- *Aborted fetuses:* stem cells are taken from fetuses in early development that have been aborted.
- *Umbilical cords:* this after-childbirth. tissue holds potential for research.
- *Adult tissue or organs:* stem cells are obtained from the tissue or organs of living adults during surgery.
- *Cadavers:* isolation and survival of neural progenitor cells from human post-mortem tissues (tip to 20 hours after death) has been reported and provides an additional source of human stem cells.

Embryonic stem cells must be obtained when an embryo is in early development, that is, when the fertilised egg has divided to form about 1000 cells. These cells are separated and maintained in a cell culture dish, thereby halting embryonic development towards creating an individual. This is why embryonic stem cell research is the subject of ethical debates. Utilisation of adult stem cells pose less of an ethical dilemma: however, adult stem cells may not have the same potential as those derived from embryos for medical therapeutics.

Comparing Embryonic and Adult Stem Cells

Embryonic stem cells have advantages and disadvantages for therepy.

Advantages

They are:

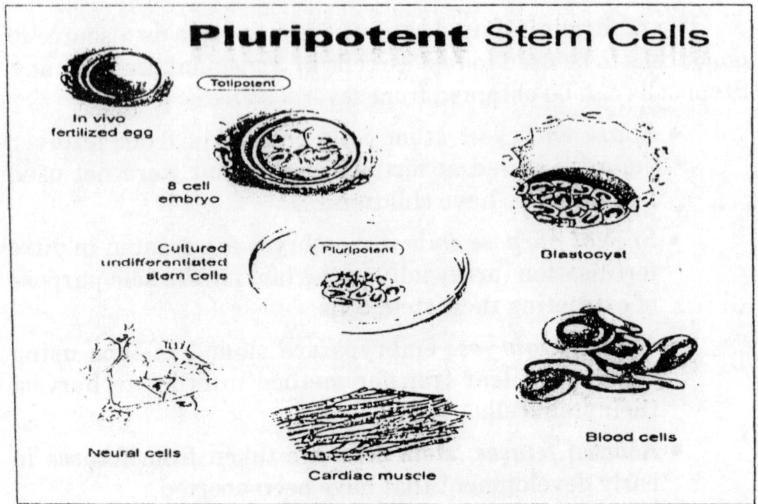

Fig. 7.3 **Pleuripotent Stem Cell**

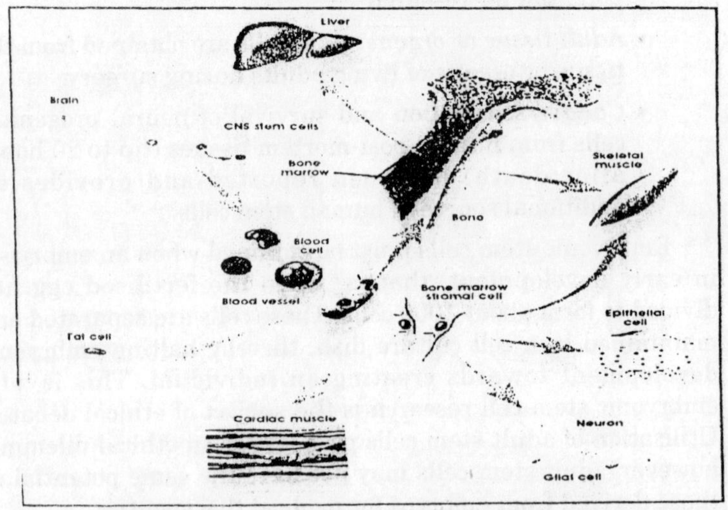

Fig. 7.4 **Pleuripotent Adult Stem Cell**

- *Flexible:* They have the potential to make any body cell.
- *Immortal:* One cell line can potentially supply endless amounts of cells with carefully defined characteristics.

- *Easily available:* human embryos can be obtained from fertility clincs.

Disadvantages

They could be:

- *Difficult to control:* The method for inducing the cell type needed to treat a particular disease must be defined and optimised.
- *At odds with a patient's immune system:* It is possible that transplanted cells would differ in their immune profile from that of the recipient and so would be rejected.
- *Ethically controversial:* Those who believe life begins at conception say that doing research on human embryos is unethical even if donors give their consent.

Adult stem cells also have good and difficult characteristics for therapy.

Advantages

They are:

- *Already somewhat specialised:* Inducement may be simpler.
- *Immune hardy:* Recipients who receive the products of their own stem cells will not experience immune rejection.
- *Flexible:* Adult stem cells may be used to form other tissue types.
- *Mixed degree of availability:* Some adult stem cells are easy to harvest and others, such as neural (brain) stem cells, can be dangerous to the donor.

Disadvantages

They could be

- *Minimal quantity:* They are difficult to obtain in large quantities.
- *Finite:* They don't live as long in a culture as embryonic stem cells.
- *Genetically unsuitable:* The harvested stem cells may carry genetic mutations for disease or become defective during experimentation.

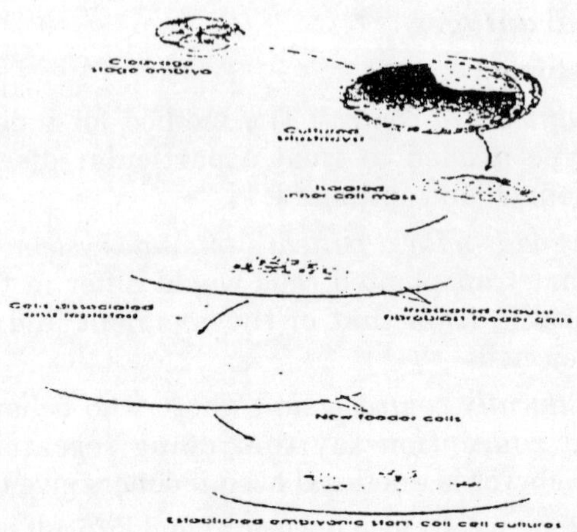

Fig. 7.5 Culture of Embryonic Stem Cell

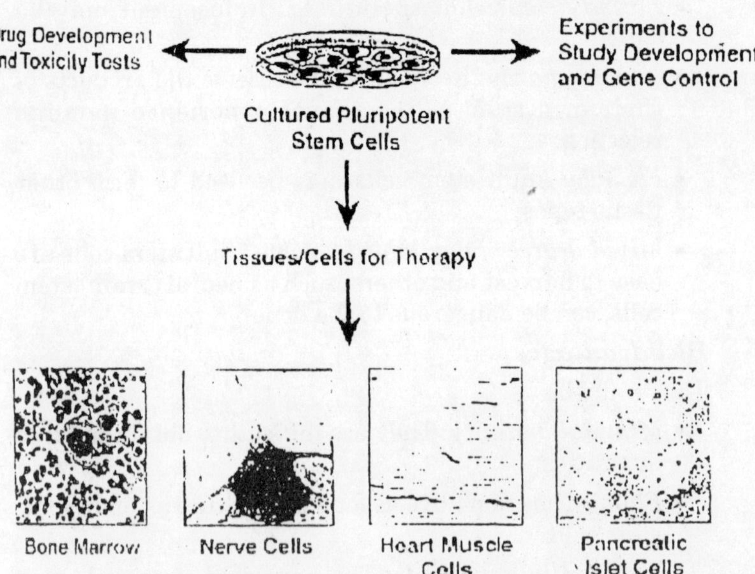

Fig. 7.6 Pluripotent Nature of Stem Cell

The Surprising Property of Adult Stem Cells: Transdifferentiation

Adult stem cells were thought to be restricted to produce differentiated cells, which were specific to the organ from which they were isolated. Recently, several examples have been reported which demonstrate that these stem cells, under certain conditions, can be induced to form other cell types (transdifferentiation). For example:

- neural stem cells (NSC) can give rise to blood and skeletal muscle
- bone marrow cells can give rise to muscle, liver cells, and astrocytes

When NSCs were used to form muscle, no inducers were needed other than co-culturing them with muscle progenitor cells (myoblasts) or injecting them into muscle.This holds promise for cell transplantation therapies in that the experiment suggests that host tissue can instruct transplanted cells to a desired result. Scientists, then, can consider whether it is best for stem cells to be differentiated *in vitro* (artificially) prior to transplantation or by transplanting them directly into the defective tissue. Some experiments have shown that naturally transplanted stem cells were able to migrate to regions where cells had died due to stroke (called ischaemia).

History of Stem Cells

1878 — The first attempt was made to fertilise mammalian eggs outside the body.

1959 — First animal made by in vitro fertilisation (IVF).

1960s — Teratocarcinomas determined to originate from embryonic germ cells in mice. Embryonal carcoinoma cells (EC) identified as a kind of stem cell.

1968 — The first human egg is fertilised in vitro.

1970s — EC cells injected into mouse blastocysts make chimeric mice. Cultured SC cells are explored as models of embryonic development in mice.

1978 — The first IVF baby is born in England.

1981 — Mouse ES cells are derived from the inner cell mass of blastocysts. Mouse ES cells are grown in vitro. ES cells injected into mice from teratomas.

1984-88 — Pluripotent, clonal cells called Embryonal Carcinoma (EC) cells are developed. When exposed to retinoic acid these cells differentiate into neuron-like cells and other cell types.

1989 — A clonal line of human embryonal carcinoma cells is derived that yields tissues from all three primary germ layers. They have limited replicative and differentiative capacity.

1994 — Human blastocysts are generated and the inner cell mass is maintained in culture. ES like cells form in the center and retain stem cell like morphology.

1995-96 — Non-human primate ES cells are maintained in vitro from the inner cell mass of monkeys. These cells are pluripotent and differentiate normally into all three primary germ layers.

1998 — ES cells from the inner cell mass of normal human blastocysts are cultured and maintained normally for many passages. EG cells are also derived and grown in vivo.

2000 — Scientists derive human ES cells from the inner cell mass of blastocysts. They proliferate in vitro for a long time and form all three germ layers and teratomas when injected into immune deficient mice.

2001 — As human ES cell lines are shared and new lines are derived, more research groups are focusing attention on the differentiation of cells *in vitro*. Many methods focus on making human tissues for transplantation.

2001 — NIH registry of human embryonic stem cell lines established, 15 Institutions and 78 cell lines were registered and eligible for US federal funding including 10 from India from two institutes.

2003 — Britain became first country to issue research licence for human embryonic cloning to create stem cells.

2004 — South Korean scientists clone 30 human embryos and develop them over several days.

2004 — UK open stem cell bank.

2005 — Dr Hwang and team from Korea develop stem cells tailored to match individual patients but shrouded with controversy.

2005 — Wisconsin scientists grows two new human embryonic stem cell lines in animal cell free culture.

The Clinical and Research Potentials for Stem Cell Products

Stem cell lines grown in the lab provide scientists with the opportunity to "engineer" them for use in transplantation or treatment of diseases. For example, before scientists can use any type of tissue, orgin, or cell for transplantation, they must overcome attempts by a patient's immune system to reject the transplant. In the future, scientists may be able to modify human stem cell lines in the laboratory by using gene therapy or other techniques to overcome this immune rejection. Scientists might also be able to replace damaged genes or add new genes to stem cells in order to give them characteristics that can ultimately treat diseases.

Stem cells have potential in many different areas of health and medical research. To start with, studying stem cells will help us to understand how they transform into the dazzling array of specialised cells that make us what we are. Some of the most serious medical conditions, such as cancer and birth defects, are due to problems that occur somewhere in this process. A better understanding of normal cell development will allow us to understand and perhaps correct the errors that cause these medical conditions.

Another potential application of stem cells is making cells and tissues for medical therapies. Today, donated organs and tissues are often used to replace those that are diseased or destroyed. Unfortunately, the number of people needing a transplant far exceeds the number of organs available for transplantation. Pluripotent stem cells offer the possibility of a renewable source of replacement cells and tissues to treat a myriad of diseases, conditions, and disabilities including Parkinson's and Alzheimer's diseases, spinal cord injury, stroke, burns, heart disease, diabetes, osteoarthritis and rheumatoid arthritis.

The economic and psychological tolls of chronic, degenerative, and acute diseases in the world are enormous. It has been estimated that up to 128 million people suffer from such diseases; thus, virtually every citizen is affected directly or indirectly. The total costs of treating diabetes, for example is approaching $100 billion in the United States alone. The condition is also not so better in our country. Most of the Indians now-a-days suffer from diseases like diabetes, cardiac stroke, inborn genetical defects and many more. As more research takes place, the developmental potential of different kinds of stem cells will become better understood. As the science is understood now, adult stem cells are limited in their potential to differentiate. Embryonic germ cells have a great' differentiation capacity, and embryonic stem cells are thought to be able to differentiate into almost any tissue. Thus, different types of stem cells could have different applications.

Some Examples of Treatments for Major Diseases

Type 1 Diabetes in Children : Type 1 diabetes is an autoimmune disease characterised by destruction of insulin producing cells in the pancreas. Current efforts to treat these patients with human islet transplantation in an effort to restore insulin secretory function (obtained from human pancreas) are limited severely by the small numbers of donated pancreas available each year combined with the toxicity of immunosuppressive drug treatments required to prevent graft rejection. Pluripotent stem cells, instructed to differentiate into a particular pancreatic cell called a beta cell, could overcome the shortage of. therapeutically effective material to transplant. They also afford the opportunity to engineer such cells to effectively resist immune attack as well as graft rejection.

Nervous System Diseases : Many nervous system diseases result from loss of nerve cells. Mature nerve cells cannot divide to replace those that are lost. Thus, without a "new" source of functioning nerve tissue, no therapeutic possibilities exist. In Parkinson's disease, nerve cells that make the chemical dopamine die. In Alzheimer's disease, cells that are responsible for the production of certain neurotransmitters die. In amyotrophic lateral sclerosis, the motor nerve cells that activate muscles die. In spinal cord injury, brain trauma, and even stroke, many different types of cells are lost or die. In multiple sclerosis,-glia, the cells that protect nerve fibers are lost. Perhaps the only hope for treating such individuals comes from the potential to create new nerve tissue restoring function from pluripotent stem cells. Remarkably, human clinical experiments have demonstrated the potential effectiveness of this approach to treatment. Parkinson's patients have been treated by surgical implantation of fetal cells into their brain with some benefit. Although not completely effective, perhaps owing to lack of sufficient numbers of dopamine secreting cells, similar experiments using appropriately differentiated stem cells should overcome those obstacles. More complex experiments have already been successfully conducted in rodent models of Parkinson's. Similar approaches could be developed to replace the dead or dysfunctional cells in cortical and hippocampal brain regions that are affected in patients with Alzheimer's.

Primary Immunodeficiency Diseases : Pluripotent stem cells could be used in treatment of virtually all primary immunodeficiency diseases. Presently, there are more than 70 different forms of congenital and inherited deficiencies of the immune system that have been recognised. These are among the most complicated diseases to treat with the worst prognoses. Included here are diseases such as severe combined immunodeficiency disease (the "bubble boy" disease), Wiskott-Aldrich Syndrome, and the autoimmune disease lupus. The immune deficiencies suffered as a result of Acquired Immuno Deficiency Syndrome (AIDS) following infection with the human immunodeficiency Virus are also relevant here. These diseases are characterised by an unusual susceptibility to infection and often associated with anaemia, arthritis, diarrhoea, and selected malignancies. However, the transplantation of stem cells reconstituted with the normal gene could result in restoration of immune function and effective normalisation of life span and quality of life for these people.

Diseases of Bone and Cartilage : Stem cells, once appropriately differentiated, could correct many diseases and degenerative conditions in which bone or cartilage: cells are deficient in numbers or defective in function. This holds promise for treatment of genetic disorders such as osteogenesis imperfecta and chondrodysplasias. Similarly, cells could be cultivated and introduced into damaged areas of joint cartilage in cases of osteoarthritis or into large gaps in bone from fractures or surgery.

Cancer : At the present time, bone marrow stem cells, representing a more committed stem cell, are used to rescue patients following high dose chemotherapy. Unfortunately, these recovered cells are limited in their capacity to restore immune function completely in this setting. It is hoped that injections of properly-differentiated stem cells would return the complete repertoire of immune response to patients undergoing bone marrow transplantation. Complete and functional restoration will be required if, for example, immune/vaccine anticancer therapy is to work. More importantly, success would permit use of very toxic (and effective) regimens that could not currently be utilised for lack of an ability to restore marrow and immuno function.

Uses in Research

Much is left to be discovered and understood all aspects of human biology. What have been frequently lacking are the tool necessary to make the initial discoveries, or to apply the knowledge of discoveries to the understanding of complex systems. These are some of the larger problems in basic and clinical biology where the use of stem cells might be the key to understanding.

A New Window on Human Developmental Biology : The story of human developmental biology is particularly constrained by practical and ethical limitations. Human ES cells may allow scientists to investigate how early human cells be the committed to the major lineages of the body; how these lineages lay down the rudiments of the body's tissues and organs; and how cells within these rudiments differentiate to form the myriad functional cell types which underlie normal function in the adult. The knowledge gained will impact many fields. For example, cancer biology will reap an especially large reward because it is now understood that many cancers arise by perturbation of normal developmental processes. The availability of human ES cells will also greatly accelerate the understanding of the causes of birth defects and thus lead directly to their possible prevention.

Models of Human Disease That are Constrained by Current Animal and Cell Culture Models : Investigation of a number of human diseases is severally constrained by a lack of *in vitro* models. A number of pathogenic viruses including human immunodeficiency virus and Hepatitis C virus grow only in human or chimpanzee cells. ES cells might provide cell and tissue types that will greatly accelerate investigation into these and other viral diseases. Current animal models of neurodegenerative diseases such as Alzheimer's disease give only a very partial representation of the disease's process.

Transplantation : Pluripotent stem cells could be used to crete an unlimited supply of cells, tissues, or even organs that could be used to restore function without the requirement for toxic immunosuppression and without regard to tissue matching compatibility. Such cells, when used in transplantation therapies, would in effect be suitable for "universal" donation. Bone marrow transplantation, a difficult and expensive procedure associated with significant hazards, could become safe, cost effective, and be available for treating a wide range of clinical disorders, including aplastic anaemia and certain inherited blood disorders. This would be especially important in persons who lost marrow function from toxic exposure, for example to radiation or toxic agents. Growth and transplant of other tissues lost to disease or accident, for example; skin, heart, nervous system components, and other major organs, are foreseeable.

Gene Therapy : In gene therapy, genetic material that provides a missing or necessary protein, or causes a clinically-relevant biochemical process, is introduced into an organ for a therapeutic effect. For gene-based therapies (specifically, those using DNA sequences), it is critical that the desired gene be introduced into organ stem cells in order to achieve long-term expression and therapeutic effect. Although techniques for delivering the therapeutic DNA have been greatly improved since the first gene therapy protocol almost 10 years ago, there are as yet no bona fide successes. Besides delivery problems, loss of expression or insufficient expression is an important limiting factor in successful application of gene therapy and could be overcome by transferring genes into stem cells.

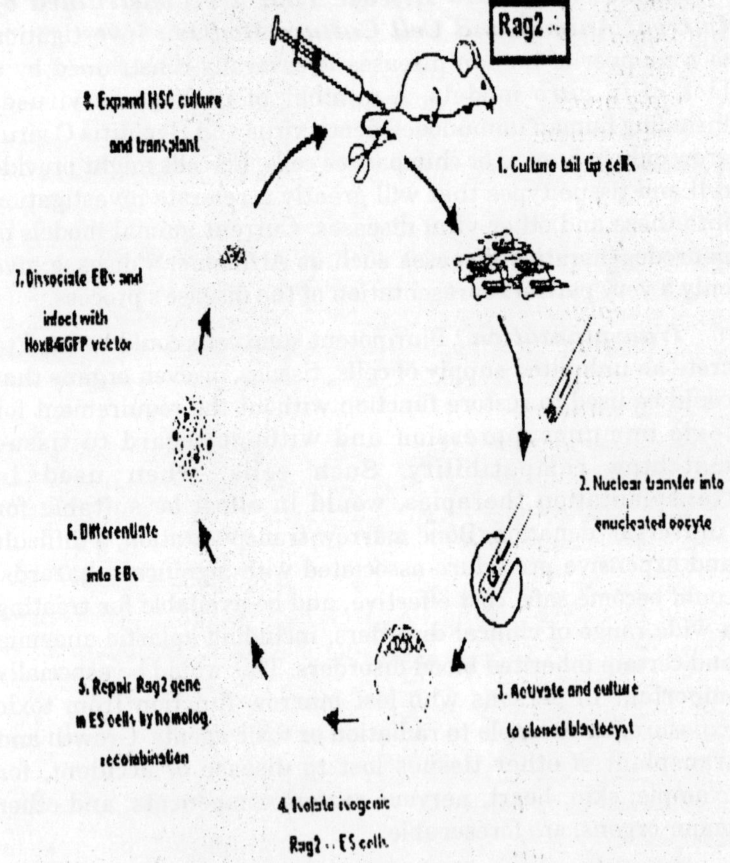

Fig. 7.7 Correction of a Genetic Defect by Combination of Therapeutic Cloning and Gene Therapy

Research opportunities and forecast: gene and stem cell therapies

Key Research Opportunities	*Forecast*
Identify Genes involved in complex diseases such as Diabetes. Obesity and Hypertension.	The propensity for a given individual to develop diseases will be understood at the molecular level. Enabling physicians to treat patients who are at greatest risk. Now molecular targets for therapeutic interventions will be elucidated.
Identify the molecular pathways underlying disease states.	Gene therapy to interfere with Pathologic Molecular Pathways theraby inhibiting disease processes.
Development of easily produced Gene Therapy Vectors capable of High-Efficency Transfer and Regulated Expression.	Gene Therapy of specific cell types for appropriate expression both temporarily and spatially to cure various diseases such as Cancer and Cardiovascular Disease.
Development of Gene Therapy Delivery Devices that are compatible with Gene Therapy Vectors and capable of targeted delivery.	Gene Therapy Vectors will be delivered through catheters directly to cells or organs of interest.
Identfy Stem Cells from different terminally different organs.	Patients with destruction of cells incapable of further division such as Cardiomyocytes of Neurons will be treated with Stem Cells to replace Lost Cells.
Identify the Molecular Pathways that regulate the plasticity of Stem Cells.	Easily isolated Stem Cells such as Bone Marrow will be treated to encourage differentiation into cells from damaged tissue such as skin for patients with burns or Neurons for patients with stoke.

Key Research Opportunities	*Forecast*
Development of technologies for efficient Nuclear Transfer of Somatic Nuclei Totipotent Stem Cells.	Stem Cells generated from Somatic Cell Nuclear will be differentiated into damaged tissue to replace Lost Cells.
Development of combined Gene and Stem Cell Therapy Approaches.	Diseased Organs that are malfunctioning due to a Genetic Mutation will be cured by harvesting the appropriate Stem Cell. Expressing the normal Gene in those cells and returning them to the individual to repopulate the entire organ.

Challenges

Stem cell research has undergone huge advances in the past couple of years. This does not mean, however, that researchers have not faced their share of problems. It has proved particularly challenging for scientists to ensure the long term proliferative ability and pluripotency of embryonic stem and germ cells.

These are important characteristics to maintain, as accurate models are necessary to understand the unique genetic and molecular basis by which these cells are able to replicate indefinitely. In addition to providing accurate models, culturing stem cells *in vitro* is also necessary in order to ensure that sufficient quantities of stem cells are available to treat specific diseases.

Teratoma formation has also produced a hurdle that needs to be overcome. Formation of these tumours like masses of cells at injection sites significantly limits the therapeutic potential applications of embryonic stem cells.

Immune challenges also prove a significant barrier to the application of stem cell therapies. If the stem cells are recognised as non-self, they will be rejected and destroyed. Two potential solutions to this problem have been proposed. One solution is the creation of universal donor stem cells through genetic engineering techniques. Theoretically stem cells could be created that lack outer surface labels. The absence of these labels, which normally identify cells as non-self, would eliminate the problem of immune rejection. Another solution to immune rejection would be to engineer stem cells identical to the recipient's cells, using the patients own DNA. The former solution of universal donor stem cells, however, would prove less labour intensive and more cost effective, than the latter solution.

Adult stem cells have also presented unique problems of their own to researchers. In addition to proving challenging to maintain in culture, like embryonic stem cells; they have proven quite rare in adult tissues. Thus adult stem cells are very difficult to isolate and identify.

India and Stem Cell Research

The stem cell research hold s great promise of improving human health by control of degenerative diseases and restoration of damage to organs by various injuries; but at the same time it also raises several ethical and social issues such as destruction of human embryos to create human embryonic stem (hES) cell lines, potential for introducing commodification in human tissues and organs with inherent barriers of access to socio-economically deprived and possible use of technology for germ-line engineering and reproductive cloning. The research in this field, therefore, needs to be regulated to strike a balance. In India stem cell research is govern and regulated by ICMR-DBT guidelines for stem cell research and therapy. The important clauses of these guidelines are as follows:

General Principles

Any research on human beings, including human embryos, as subjects of medical or scientific research or experimentation, shall adhere to the general principles outlined in the "Ethical guidelines for Biomedical Research on Human Subjects" issued by the Indian Council of Medical Research (ICMR) in October, 2000 (www.icmr.nic.in/bioethics). The same in brief are enumerated below:

- Essentiality of research with potential health benefits;
- Respect for human dignity, human rights and fundamental freedoms;
- Individual autonomy with respect to informed consent, privacy and confidentiality in harmony with the individual's cultural sensitivity and environment;
- Justice with equitable distribution of burden and benefits;
- Beneficence with regard to improvement of health of individuals and society;
- Non-malificence with the aim of minimisation of risk and maximisation of benefit;
- Freedom of conducting research with due respect to the above within the regulatory framework.

Permissible Areas of Research

- *In vitro* studies on established cell lines from any type of stem cell viz. hES, hEG, hSS or fetal/adult stem cells may be carried out with notification to ICSCRT, provided the cell line is registered with the IC-SCRT/ NAC-SCRT and GLP is followed.
- *In vivo* studies with established cell lines from any type of stem cells *viz.*, hES, hEG, hSS, including differentiated derivatives of these cells, *on adult animals other than primates* with prior approval of IC-SCRT, provided such animals are not allowed to breed. This includes pre-clinical evaluation of efficacy and safety of human stem cell lines.
- *In vivo* studies on experimental animals (other than primates) using *fetal/adult somatic stem cells* from Bone marrow, peripheral blood, umbilical cord blood.cells, dental cells, bone cells, cartilage cells or any other organ (including placenta), with prior approval of the IC-SCRT and IEC provided appropriate consent is obtained from the donor as per guidelines provided in this document.

- Establishment of new hES cell lines from spare, supernumerary embryos with prior approval of the IC-SCRT and IEC provided appropriate consent is obtained from the donor as per guidelines given below. Once the cell line is established it shall be registered with the IC-SCRT and NAC-SCRT.
- Establishment of fetal/adult hSS cell lines with prior approval of the IC-SCRT and IEC provided appropriate consent is obtained from the donor as per guidelines provided in this document.
- Establishment of Umbilical Cord stem cell bank with prior approval of the ICSCRT and IEC provided guidelines given in this document for collection, processing, and storage etc of the umbilical cord blood are followed. Appropriate SOPs shall be approved by the IC-SCRT and IEC.
- Clinical trial with clinical grade stem cells, following ICMR Guidelines for Biomedical Research and GCP guidelines of the GOI, may be carried out with prior approval of IC-SCRT, IEC and DCGI. Clinical grade stem cells are required to be produced under international GMP/GTP conditions. All clinical trials on stem cells shall be registered with NAC-SCRT through IC-SCRT.

Restricted Areas of Research

- Creation of a zygote by IVF, SCNT or any other method with the specific aim of deriving a hES cell line for any purpose. Specific justification would be required to consider the request for approval by the NAC-SCRT through IEC and IC-SCRT. It would be required to establish that creation of zygote is critical and essential for the proposed research, and no other alternative will serve the purpose. Informed consent procedure for donation of ova, sperm, somatic cell or other as detailed in these guidelines would need to be followed.

- Clinical trials sponsored by multinationals, involving stem cell products imported from abroad. Such collaboration shall require prior approval of the NAC-SCRT through IC-SCRT, IEC,DCGI and respective funding agency as per its procedure/Health Ministry's Screening Committee (HMSC).
- Research involving introduction of hES/hEG/hSS cells into animals, including primates, at embryonic or fetal stage of development for studies on pattern of differentiation and integration of human cells into non-human animal tissues. If there is a possibility that human cells could contribute in a major way to the development of brain or gonads of the recipient animal, the scientific justification for the experiments must be strong. *The animals derived from these experiments shall not be allowed to breed.* Such proposals would need approval of the NAC-SCRT through Animal IEC and IC-SCRT.
- Studies on chimeras where stem cells from two or more species are mixed and introduced into animals, including primates, at any stage of development *viz.*, embryonic, fetal or postnatal, for studies on pattern of development and differentiation.
- Research in which the identity of the donors of blastocysts, gametes, or somatic cells from which the hES cells were derived is readily ascertainable or might become known to the investigator.

Prohibited Areas of Research

- Any research related to germ line genetic engineering or reproductive cloning.
- Any *in vitro* culture of intact human embryo, regardless of the method of its derivation, beyond 14 days or formation of primitive streak, whichever is earlier.
- Transfer of human blastocysts generated by SCNT or parthenogenetic orandrogenetic techniques into a human or non-human uterus.

- Any research involving implantation of human embryo into uterus after *in vitro* manipulation, at any stage of development, in humans or primates.
- Animals in which any of human stem cells have been introduced at any stage of development should not be allowed to breed.
- Research involving directed non-autologous donation of any stem cells to a particular individual is also prohibited.

Research Using Umbilical Cord Blood Stem Cells

Cord blood stem cell banking is permissible. All Cord blood banks have to be registered with the Drug Controller General of India (DCGI) as per the guidelines of blood banks. Purpose of banking should be clearly explained to couples interested in storing cord blood. The ethical issues include concern about ownership and risk of transmission of potential genetic disorders, besides other general issues of confidentiality, justice and beneficence. When it comes to registries and banking, the commercial aspects pose additional problems. The advertising involved in getting and collecting samples, conflict of interest, utility of samples, accessibility and affordability should also be carefully looked into. The following points should be considered while collecting umbilical cord blood as specified in "Ethical Guidelines for Biomedical Research in Human Subjects"

2000 of ICMR:

- No harm should occur to the fetus or the neonate.
- Exact timing of the clamping of the umbilical cord should be defined in the clamping protocol.
- Parents should be informed regarding risks and benefits involved.
- Free informed consent from parents' should be obtained. If there is disagreement between the parents, the mother's wish shall prevail.
- ID card should be issued for voluntary donation to enable access/benefit in future in case required for self/ relative.

- Standard Operative Procedures for collection, transportation, processing, storage, preservation and clinical use should be laid down with approval of the IC-SCRT and IEC.
- Detailed protocol for isolation and characterisation of stem cells should be approved by IC-SCRT and IEC.
- Period of preservation for self- use later in life should be prescribed.
- Detailed protocol for clinical use of stem cells should be in place.
- Follow-up plans for assessing safety and efficacy of cord blood stem cell therapy should be incorporated.

Research Using Fetal Stem Cells/Placenta

All proposals involving fetuses or fetal tissue, for research or therapy are permissible. However,

- Termination of pregnancy should not be sought with a view to donate fetal tissue in return for possible financial or therapeutic benefits.
- Consent to have a termination of pregnancy and the donation of fetal material for purpose of research or therapy should be taken separately.
- The medical person responsible for the care of the pregnant woman planning to undergo termination of pregnancy and the person who will be using the fetal material should not be the same.
- The women shall not have the option to specify the use for a particular person or in a particular way.
- The identity of the donor and the recipient should be kept confidential.

Use of Stem Cells for Therapeutic Purposes

- As of date, there is no approved indication for stem cell therapy as a part of routine medical practice, other than Bone Marrow Transplantation (BMT).
- Accordingly all stem cell therapy other than BMT (for accepted indications) shall be treated as experimental.

It should be conducted only as clinical trial after approval of the IEC, IC-SCRT and DCGJ. All such trials shall be registered with the NAC-SCRT.

- Only clinical grade stem cells/cell lines shall be used for stem cell clinical trials. These should meet the standards of GTP/GMP adopted by international tissue banks. As far as possible the use of animal products such as calf serum/feeder layer etc. for derivation and maintenance of cell lines shall be avoided.
- The injectible product should meet pharmacopia I specifications for parenteral preparations. As far as possible the cells used for therapy shall be free from animal products and microbial contamination.
- The centers carrying out stem cell clinical trials, and the source providing clinical grade stem cells/cell lines for the trial' shall be registered/accredited with the NAC-SCRT (hrough IC-SCRT. In case of International Collaboration the NAC-SCRT shall ensure that the certification provided by the collaborating country fulfills the requirements laid down in these guidelines.

Conclusion

There exists a widespread controversy over stem cell research, which emanates from the techniques used in the creation and usage of stem cells. In particular, research using embryonic stem cells has proven to be an immensely sensitive topic. This is because, with the present state of technology, starting a stem cell 'line' requires the destruction of a human embryo and/or therapeutic cloning. Opponents of the research argue that this practice is a slippery slope to reproductive cloning and tantamount to the objectification of a potential human being. Contrarily, medical researchers in the field argue that it is necessary to pursue embryonic stem cell research because the resultant technologies are expected to have significant medical potential. The ensuing debate has prompted national and international authorities to seek suitable regulatory frameworks and highlighted the fact that stem cell research represents a moral, social and ethical minefield.

Human stem cell research holds enormous potential for contributing to our understanding of fundamental human biology. Although it is not possible to predict the outcomes from basic research, such studies will offer the real possibility for treatments and ultimately for cures for many diseases for which adequate therapies do not exist.

The pursuit and production of knowledge through scientific research is an undertaking that offers enormous intellectual rewards for researchers while also performing an important social function. The advancement of science has transformed our lives in ways that would have been unpredictable just a half-century ago. Whether stem cell research will have a similar effect remains to be determined, but the promise is so great that it seems wise to consider seriously how best to further such research in a manner that is sensitive to public sensibilities. Public conversations about research and use of human stem cells are well underway. Science does not exist in isolation from the larger community that feels its effects, whether perceived as good or bad. The work of scientists is, and should be, conditioned and directed by consideration of broader human values. This means that the development of public policy, especially where highly controversial matters are involved, must take all interred sectors of the public into account. It is only through broad-based participation that the values of all stakeholders in the stem cell research enterprise can be carefully considered and weighed.

References

1. National Institutes of Health, "Stem Cell Basics", July 19, 2004.
2. Vacanti MP, Roy A, Cortiella J, Bonassar L, Vacanti CA (2001). "Identification and Initial Characterisation of Spore-like Cells in Adult Mammals". *J Cell Biochem* 80 (3): 455-60, PMID 11135375.
3. National Institutes of Health, Stem Cell FAQ, April 13, 2005.
4. Graham, Judith and Schodolski, Vincent J., "Son of Former President Reagan Enters the Fray with a Speech at the Democratic Convention." Chicago Tribune, July 27, 2004.
5. Wicha MS, Liu S, Dontu G (2006). "Cancer Stem Cells: An Old Idea—A Paradigm Shift." *Cancer Res* 66: 1883-90. PMID 16488983.

6. Bonnet D, Dick JE (1997). "Human Acute Myeloid Leukemia is Organised as a Hierarchy that Originates from a Primitive Hematopoietic Cell." *Nat Med* 3: 730-7. 9212098.

7. Thomson, J.A., Waknitz, M.A., Swiergiel, J.J., and Marshall, V.S., "Embryonic Stem Cell Lines Derived from Human Blastocysts." *Sceince*, 282: 1061-1062 (1998).

8. Thomas Okarma (Geron Corporation), AAAS Public Forum on Stem Cell Research Issues (25 August 1999).

9. Shamblott, M.J., Axelman, J., Wang, S., Bugg., E.M., Littlefield, J.W., Donovan, P.J., Blumenthal, P.D., Huggins, G.R., and Gearhart, J.D. "Derivation of Pluripotent Stem Cells from Cultured Human Primordial Germ Cells." *Proceedings of the National Academy of Sciences*, 95: 13726-13731 (1998).

10. Kato, Y., Rideout, W.M., Hilton, K., Barton, S.C., Tsunoda, Y., and Surani, M.A. "Developmental Potential of Mouse Primordial Germ Cells." *Development 126:* 1823-1832 (1999).

11. Pittenger, M.F., Mackay, A.M., Beck, S.C., Jaiswal, R.K., Douglas, R., Mosca, J., Moorman, M., Simonetti, D., Craig, S., and Marshak, D.R., "Multilineage Potential of Mesenchymal Stem Cells." *Science, 284:* 143-147 (1999).

12. Schierle, G.S., Hansson, O., Leist, M., Nicotera, P., Widner, H., and Brundin, P., "Caspase Inhibition Reduces Aoptosis and Increases Survival of Nigral Transplants." *Nature Medicine 5:* 97-100 (1999).

13. Shannon, T.A., and Walter, A.B., "Reflections on the Moral Status of the Pre-Embryo." *Theological Studies* 51: 603-26 (1990).

14. Cahill, L.S., "The Embryo and the Fetus: New Moral Contexts." *Theological Studies* 54: 124-42 (1993).

15. Siegel, S., "Fetal Experimentation" in *Contemporary Jewish Ethics* (Kellner, M., Ed.) 289 (1978).

16. Nagy, A., Rossant, J., Nagy, R., Abromow-Newerly, W., and Roder, J.C., "Derivation of Completely Cell Culture-derived Mice from Early-passage Embryonic Stem Cells." *Proceedings of the National Academy of Sciences* 90: 8424-8428 (1993).

8

ENVIRONMENTAL POLLUTION BY HEAVY METAL CADMIUM: TOXIC EFFECTS ON RNA CONTENT OF A FRESH WATER FISH, *OREOCHROMIS MOSSAMBICUS*, PETERS

Dr. Lngaraj Patro *

Dr. Minati Mahapatra **

Dr. S.C. Swain*

ABSTRACT

Heavy metal cadmium compounds discharged from different industries into water bodies are having detrimental effects on aquatic species such as fishes. In this paper an attempt has been made to study the toxic effects of heavy metal cadmium on a fresh water fish, *Oreochromis mossambicus,* Peters and its ecological implications. It has been observed that cadmium chloride exposed fishes appeared lethargic when compared to control fish. Inappetence and ataxia was observed in exposed fish. Exposed fishes showed erratic movements loss of equilibrium, gradual onset of inactivity etc. Significant change in RNA content was noted in muscle and liver tissues of exposed fish. Least difference was noted in the exposed brain tissue, when compared to control. No recovery in RNA content was noted in the exposed brain tissue, rather the per cent

* Laboratory of Environmental Toxicology, Department of Zoology, Aska Science College, Aska, 761111 (Orissa), E-mail: dr.lingarajpatra@sify.com, Mob-09337739823.

** Laboratory of Plant Physiology and Bio-Chemistry, Department of Botany, Science College Hinjilicut, (Orissa).

*** Krishi Bijyan Kendra Rayagada, (OUAT) AT/PO-Gunupur Pin-765022 (Orissa) decrease increased during recovery period, partial recovery by 5.1 per cent and 9.2 per cent was observed in the fish liver and muscle during recovery period.

Key Words: Fish, Cadmium Chloride, RNA content, Brain, Liver, Muscle tissues.

Introduction

Heavy metal contamination caused by either natural process or by human activities is one of the most serious eco-toxicological problems (Reddy and Prasad, 1990). Cadmium is one of the most toxic metals occurring in nature. There is ample evidence in the literature that this metal is highly toxic to all living organisms (Yannai and Berdicevsky, 1995). In human chronic exposure to cadmium causes severe damage to the kidneys and it has been linked to enhanced ageing process, as well as cancer (Jentsch *et.al.*, 1993). Due to many industrial uses such as an electroplating plants, dyestuffs industries and metallurgy and mining industries. This metal, cadmium has become widely employed and is now a major threat to man's environment. Numerous studies have demonstrated that the organic derivatives of metals are by far more toxic than their inorganic ions (Iverson and Brinckman, 1978).Further the organic derivatives of heavy metals posses a much higher capability for absorption and accumulation in animal bodies, than the inorganic ions (Venugopal and Lucky, 1978; Nakajima and Sakaguchi, 1986 : Gadd, 1990). Little information is available on the formation of organic derivatives of cadmium by environmental process. Toxicants effects on growth may be studied by examining macro molecules involved in growth, such as DNA, RNA and Protein (Barren and Adelman 1984). However, toxicant induced changes in macro molecular content (RNA, DNA and Protein) and RNA/DNA, RNA/Protein and Protein/DNA ratio have received very little attention in fish (Barren and Adelman 1984). Kearns and Atchison 1979 correlated RNA/DNA of young of the year yellow perch to growth rate and cadmium concentration in a metal contaminated lake. Mudge *et al.,* 1977 found reduced cell size and decreased cytoplasmic RNA content in the internal tissue of *brooke trout* acutely exposed to acid stress. Stroganov, 1977 reported that cadmium of to lethal concentrations, did not affect RNA or DNA tissue content.

Keeping in view, the availability of heavy metal cadmium in the environment and discharge of industrial wastes of some industry containing cadmium compounds, entry of these chemicals into water bodies of the locality along with the irrigated water or run off water in the rainy season, availability of cadmium in the air and consequent precipitation and entry of rain run off water into water bodies and their possible effects on the fresh water fishes surviving in the water bodies, this project was masterminded to evaluate the toxicological effects of cadmium on the RNA content of a fresh water fish, *Oreochromis mossambicus,* Peters.

Material and Methods

Oreochromis mossambicus, Peters of medium size (30-35 g) were collected from the local nursery of Fisheries Department of Berhampur (Ganjam), Orissa. The Fishes were allowed to grow in the laboratory reservoirs for acclimatisation at least for 30 days before starting the experiment. The fishes were maintained in the aquarium, chlorine free tap water was used in both control and experimental aquarium. The water was changed daily. Air was bubbled through water of the aquarium to maintain the dissolved oxygen at 85 ± 5 per cent air saturation value. Living earthworm from garden showing no contamination by any toxicant were collected and feed daily to both control and exposed fishes initially and slowly the diet of boiled eggs during holding thoughout the experimental exposure and recovery period. After acclimatisation, the fishes were washed thoroughly with 1 per cent dilute potassium permanganate ($KMnO_4$) solution, so as to prevent any infection the test solution of the experimental aquarium was changed daily so as to maintain the constancy of the heavy metal concentration. The experimental aquarium washed thoroughly to remove any amount of heavy metal adhered to glass surface. Exposed fishes were observed daily to record any change in behaviour, when compared to control fishes. The test fishes, *Oreochromis mossambicus* were collected acclimatised in the laboratory as described above. A graded series of concentrations of cadmium chloride ranging from 0.5 mg. 1^{-1} to 1.5 mg. 1^{-1}

were prepared. 10 healthy fishes were exposed to each concentration in 10 liter glass jars. The experiments were conducted in chlorine-free tap water at a room temperature of 26 ± 2°C. The mortality rate of test fishes were studied following the method described by Shaw (1987). Observation on the toxicity of cadmium chloride was made at 24, 48, 72, 96, hours and 28 days after the experimental animals were first exposed individuals showing no respiratory movements, no opercular movements and no response to a tactile stimulus were recorded as dead, and were immediately removed. The test fishes exposed to lower range of the cadmium chloride was exposed for a period 5 weeks to find out the maximum allowable concentration (MAC), where no mortality was noticed and this was expressed as mg. 1^{-1}.

Biochemical Analysis

The test fishes were sacrificed at 7 days interval (both control and exposed). Brain, liver and muscle tissues were removed carefully and kept in watch glasses and weight separately. Care was taken to avoid contamination during autopsy. The tissues were taken and processed for studying the change in RNA content in brain, liver, and muscle of fishes exposed to cadmium chloride at sub-lethal concentration.

100 mg. of the tissue was taken and homogenised with 5 ml of 70 per cent alcohol in micro tissue homogeniser and then centrifuged. The residue after centrifugation was then suspended in 5ml of Ethanol and Ether (1 : 1) for 10 minutes and centrifuged. The supernatant was discarded. The residue was taken and heated on boiling water bath for 30 minutes with 5ml of 0.5 N Perchloric acid. The residue was rejected. The supernatant was taken for RNA analysis. 2 ml. of the supernatant was taken and 3 ml. of the Oricinol reagent was added and heated at 80°C. for 30 minutes and cooled. The optical density was measured in a spectrophotometer. The amount of RNA was calculated from the standard graph, where RNA (Sigma) was taken as standard (Volkin and Conn, 1954). The concentrations of RNA in tissues were expressed as mg. g^{-1} of wet tissue.

Results

The MAC value of cadmium chloride was found to be 1.05 mg. l^{-1} for 30 days and to be on the safe side 1.00 mg. l^{-1} was considered for 28 days of the exposure for the study of RNA content. The major clinical symptoms such as inappetence and ataxia appeared after 2 to 3 days exposure. The other sign of toxicity such as loss of equilibrium, gradual unset of inactivity, erratic swimming with irregular collision to the inner glass walls of the aquarium was observed.

Change in RNA content in control and cadmium chloride exposed brain, liver and muscle tissues at different days of exposure and recovery has been presented in *Fig. 8.1* to *8.6* and *table 8.1* and *8.2*. The RNA content in brain tissue declined from 3.74 ± 0.21 to 2.88 ± 0.14 mg. g^{-1} dry tissue after 28 days of exposure showing a maximum depletion of 22.9%, when compared to control value (*Table 8.1* and *8.2, Fig. 8.1* to *8.5*). When the exposed fish was transferred to toxicant free medium for recovery studies, no recovery was marked. Rather depletion of RNA content was marked. During recovery studies, the RNA content declined from 3.75 ± 0.12 to 2.58 ± 0.11 mg. g^{-1} dry tissue after 28 days recovery (*Fig. 8.5*). The RNA content decreased by 0.8% on 7th day, by 0.5% on 14th day, by 3.7% on 21st day and by 22.9% on 28th day (*Fig. 8.4*). The RNA content in liver tissue declined from 4.12 ± 0.12 to 2.74 ± 0.14 mg. g^{-1} dry tissue after 28 days of exposure showing a maximum depletion of 33.4%, when compared to the control value (*Table 8.1* & *8.2 Fig. 8.2*). When the exposed fish was transferred to toxicant free medium for recovery studies, no partial recovery was marked. Though depletion of RNA content continued but the per cent of decrease was less when compared to 28th day exposure period value. During recovery studies, the RNA content declined from 4.14 ± 0.13 to 2.81 ± 0.14 mg. g^{-1} dry tissue after 14th days of recovery and the macro molecular content depleted from 4.16 ± 0.12 to 2.98 ± 0.16 mg. g^{-1} dry tissue after 28 days of recovery (*Fig. 8.2* and *8.4*). The RNA content declined by 32.1% and 28.3% on 14th and 28th day of recovery respectively. The RNA content increased by 14.7% on 7th day, by 7.2% on 14th day and decreased by 27.4% on 21st day and by 33.4% on 28th day of exposure (*Fig. 8.4*).

Table 8.1 **Changes in total RNA content (mg. g^{-1} dry weight) in control and exposed fish brain, liver and muscle at different days of exposure and recovery. (Data are the mean of 3 samples ± standard deviation).**

Tissue	Condition	Exposure in days					Recovery in days	
		0	7	14	21	28	14	28
Brain	Control	3.74 ± 0.12	3.74 ± 0.11	3.74 ± 0.05	3.75 ± 0.22	3.74 ± 0.21	3.75 ± 0.15	3.75 ± 0.12
	Exposed	3.74 ± 0.12	3.71 ± 0.08	3.72 ± 0.14	3.16 ± 0.22	2.88 ± 0.14	2.64 ± 0.12	2.58 ± 0.11
Liver	Control	4.10 ± 0.14	4.13 ± 0.14	4.16 ± 0.12	4.19 ± 0.08	4.12 ± 0.12	4.14 ± 0.13	4.16 ± 0.12
	Exposed	4.10 ± 0.14	4.74 ± 0.13	4.46 ± 0.11	3.04 ± 0.09	2.74 ± 0.14	2.81 ± 0.14	2.98 ± 0.16
Muscle	Control	4.31 ± 0.11	4.32 ± 0.15	4.33 ± 0.14	4.32 ± 0.15	4.32 ± 0.13	4.33 ± 0.12	4.34 ± 0.11
	Exposed	4.31 ± 0.11	4.11 ± 0.24	3.27 ± 0.19	2.16 ± 0.11	1.94 ± 0.14	2.12 ± 0.12	2.35 ± 0.14

Table 8.2 **Per cent change in RNA content in exposed fish brain, liver and muslce at different exposure and recovery period, when compared to respective controls. Values in parentheses indicate per cent recovery. (Data calculated from the mean of the samples).**

Tissue	Exposure in days					Recovery in days	
	0	7	14	21	28	14	28
Brain	0.0	–0.8	–0.5	–3.7	–22.9	–29.6 (NR)	–31.2 (NR)
Liver	0.0	+14.7	+7.2	–27.4	–33.4	–32.1 (1.3)	–28.3 (5.1)
Muscle	0.0	–4.8	–24.4	–50.0	–55.0	–51.0 (4.0)	–45.8 (9.2)

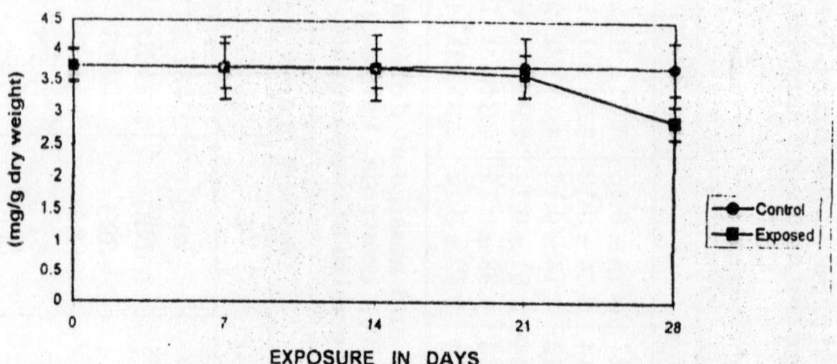

Fig. 8.1 Changes in RNA content of brain of control and exposed fish at different exposure periods

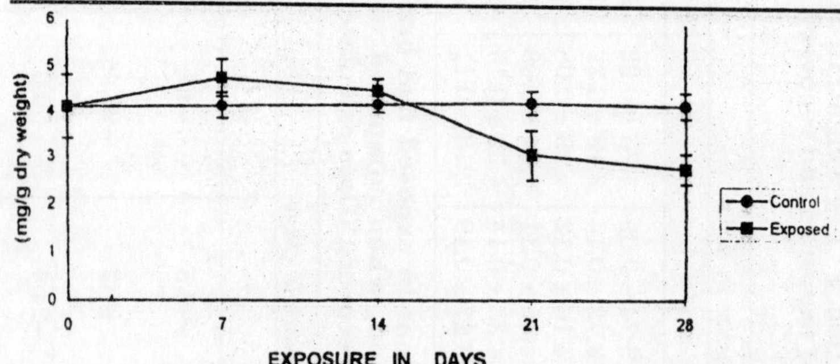

Fig. 8.2 Changes in RNA content of liver of control and exposed fish at different exposure periods

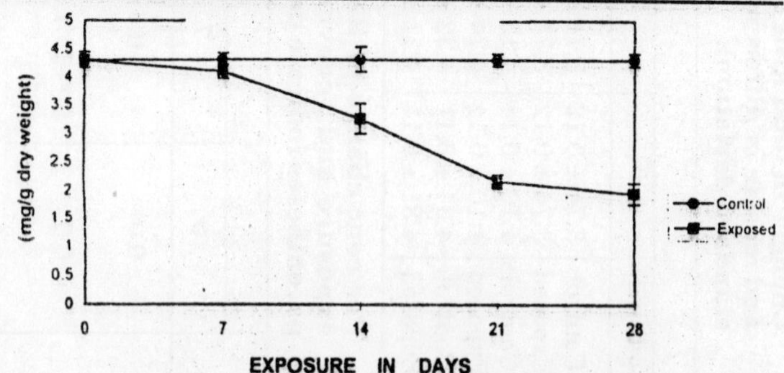

Fig. 8.3 Changes in RNA content of muscle of control and exposed fish at different expsoure periods

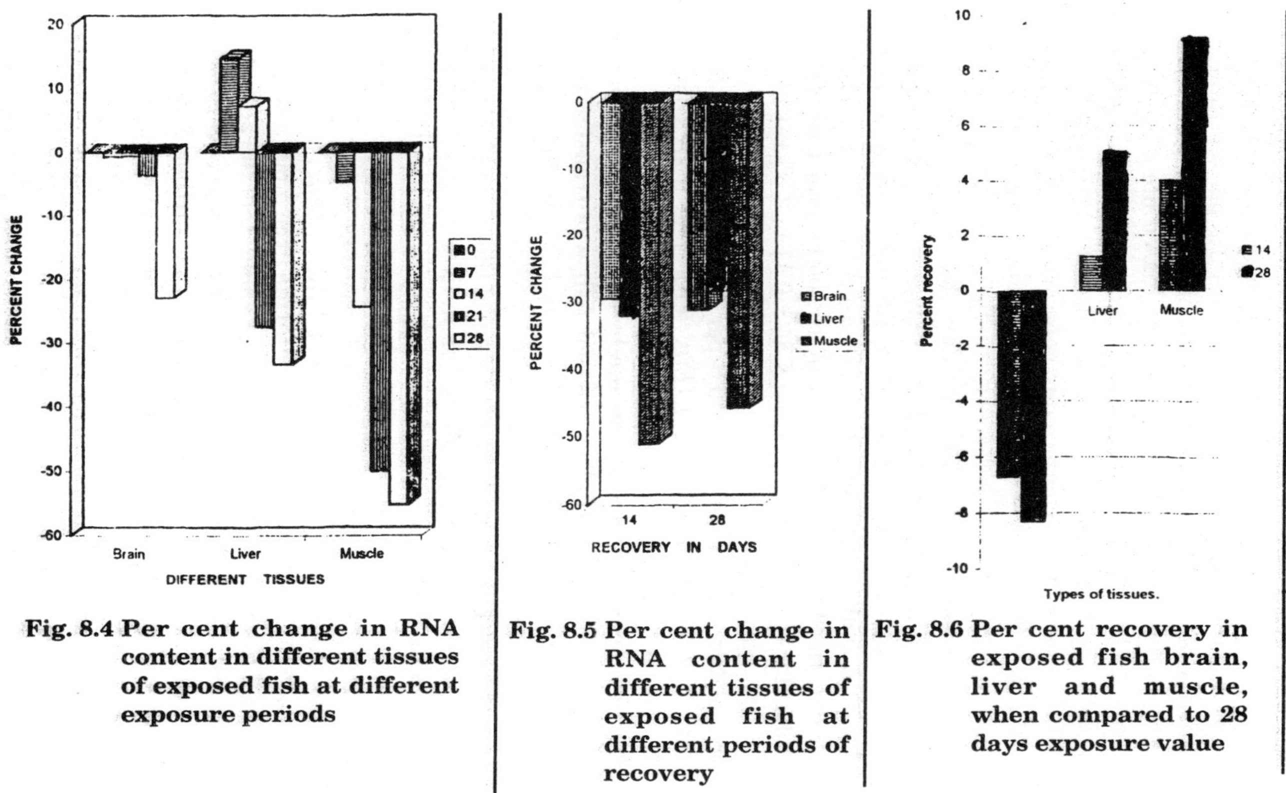

Fig. 8.4 Per cent change in RNA content in different tissues of exposed fish at different exposure periods

Fig. 8.5 Per cent change in RNA content in different tissues of exposed fish at different periods of recovery

Fig. 8.6 Per cent recovery in exposed fish brain, liver and muscle, when compared to 28 days exposure value

The exposed fish was transferred to toxicant free medium for recovery studies. On 14th day of recovery 1.3 per cent and on 28th day of recovery 5.1 per cent was observed in exposed liver tissue of the exposed fish (*Fig. 8.6*). The RNA content in muscle tissue declined from 4.32 ± 0.13 to 1.94 ± 0.14 mg. g^{-1} dry tissue after 28 days of exposure showing a maximum depletion of 55 per cent, when compared to control value (*Table 8.1, 8.2 and Fig. 8.3, 8.4*). When the exposed fish was transferred to toxicant free medium for recovery studies, insignificant partial recovery was marked. Though depletion of RNA content continued but the per cent of decrease was less when compared to 28th day exposure period value. During recovery studies, the RNA content declined from 4.33 ± 0.12 to 2.12 ± 0.12 mg. g^{-1} dry tissue after 14th days of recovery and the macro molecular content depleted from 4.34 ± 0.11 to 2.35 ± 0.14 mg. g^{-1} dry tissue after 28 days of recovery. The RNA content declined by 51 per cent and 45.8 per cent on 14th and 28th day of recovery respectively (*Fig. 8.5*). The RNA content decreased by 4.8 per cent on 7th day, by 24.4 per cent on 14th day by 50 per cent on 21st day and by 55 per cent on 28th day of exposure (*Fig. 8.4*). The exposed fish was transferred to toxicant free medium for recovery studies. On 14th day of recoery 4 per cent and on 28th day of recovery 9.2 per cent was observed in exposed muscle tissue of the exposed fish (*Fig. 8.6*). The brain was least affected than liver and muscle (*Fig. 8.1 to 8.6*). With the increase in exposure period, the RNA content declined significantly at higher exposure periods (*Table 8.1 and 8.2*). A partial insignificant recovery was marked in all the three tissue studied except brain tissue, when the exposed fish was to cadmium chloride free medium. The exposed brain showed decrease in the value from the 28th day exposure value after 28 day of recovery. No recovery was marked in the exposed brain tissue, rather further depletion in RNA content was noted. The RNA content of exposed liver recovered by 9.2 per cent only after 28th day of recovery. Hence, no significant variation was marked during recovery period. From the observation and from recovery studies, it is evident that the cadmium chloride induces permanent damage, where 100 per cent recovery was not possible under experimental condition. The exposed liver showed a negative significant correlation with the exposure period. Two way analysis of variance ratio test based on *table 8.1 and 8.2*, pertaining to change and per cent decrease in RNA content in exposed fish indicated the existence of non-significant difference between rows and significant between columns. The correlation coefficient analysis between days of exposure and change in the RNA content of brain of the control fish, showed non-significant correlation. The RNA content of exposed fish muscle showed a negative significant correlation with the exposer period. Whereas, the RNA content of exposed fish liver showed a significant negative correlation with the exposure period. Two way analysis of variance ratio test based on *table 8.1 and 8.2*, pertaining to change and per cent change in RNA content in brain, lever and muscle of exposed fish indicated the existence of a significant difference between rows and columns.

Discussion

The existence of a close quantitative relationship between RNA content and protein synthesis was pointed out by Caldwell *et.al.,* 1950 in cultures of micro organisms. Priece 1952 showed the existence of an excellent correlation between the synthesis of RNA and synthesis of proteins. Toxicant affect on macro molecular content is often due to an indirect action on nucleic acid and protein synthesis, since a toxicant that interferes with energy yielding reactions is directly an inhibitor of the synthesis of RNA, DNA and protein (Holbrook, 1980 and Barron and Adelman 1984). The observation indicated that with the increase in exposure period the DNA, RNA and protein content decrease significantly. Free amino acid content indicated a negative correlation with exposure period. The data are totally agreement with the findings of Panigrahi 1984 and Harichandan 2002. Liver being the active site of all metabolic functions, it place a crucial role in biotransformation of toxic agents (Bruin 1976). The decrease in RNA content in lever, brain and muscle of exposed fish was most probably due to an increased RNA breakdown (Ahuja and Subrahmanyam—1978) reported a decline in RNA content in the brain cells due to nervous over excitation induced by prolonged training. Since structural RNA constitutes more than 80 per cent of the total

RNA content (Ahuja and Subrahmanyam—1978) the decline in RNA content could be most probably due decrease in structural RNA which not reflect change in protein content. The excessive loading of cadmium and other heavy metals in recent years tend to contaminate the environment. Controversy has centered around both the mode of action of toxicants in affecting plant and animal metabolism and the extent of its toxicity resulting from penetration into the biological system. The heavy metal pollution was not a big problem for pretty long time in India. But the recent awareness and environmental impact assessment programmes conducted by different pollution control boards, department of environment and forest of both state and Center environmental monitoring and status reports forced every one to think about the environment and its protection.

References

Ahuja A.K. and Subrahmanyam D., (1978): Pros. Indian Acad. Sci. 87(8) 189.

Barren M.G. and Adelman I. R. 1984 : Nuclic Acid, Protein Content and Growth of Larval Fish Sub Lethally Exposed to Various Toxicants. Can, J. Fish Aquat Sci, 41 : 141.

Bruin A. De 1976 : Nuclic Acid Metabolism in Biochemical Toxicity of Environmental Agents. Ed. Bruin A. De. pp. 605-655, Elsevier/ North Holland Biomedical Press. The Netherlands.

Caldwell. P.C., E.L. Mackor and C. Hinshelwood 1950 : J. Chem. Soc. 31: 51.

Gadd G.M. (1990): Heavy Metal Accumulation by Bacteria and Other Microorganisms. Experimental, 46: 834-839.

Harichandan N.L. 2002 : Toxicological Effects of Cadmium Chloride Contained Effluent on a Fresh Water Fish and Its Ecological Significance Ph.D. Thesis, Berhampur University, Orissa.

Holbrook D.J. Jr. (1980): Effects of Toxicants on Nucleic Acid and Protein Metabolism. p. 261-284 . In. E. Hodgson and F.E. Guthrie (Ed). Introduction ot Biochemical Toxicology, Elsevier, New York.

Iverson W. and Brinckman F.F., 1978 : Microvial Metabolism of Heavy Metals in Water Pollutions Microbiology (R. Mitachell, Ed.) Vol. 2, pp. 201-232 Wily, New York.

Jentsch S., Schobertic, Reins H.A. and Jungman,1993: Resistance to Cadmium Mediated by Ubiquitin-dependent Protolysis Nature, 361; 369-371 Kearns and Atchison 1979.

Nakagima A. and Sakaguchi T., 1986 : Selective Accumulation of Heavy Metals by Microorganisms. Appl. Microbiol. Biotechnol. 24, 59-64.

Panigrahi A.K. 1984 : Eco-physiological Effects on Mercurial Compounds on Some Fresh Water Fish (Toxicological Effects of Inorganic Mercury ($Hg(NO_3)_2$) on two fresh water fish, Tilapia Mossambica, Pters and Anabas Scandens Cuv and Val and Its Ecological Implications, Ph. D. Thesis, Berhampur University.

Reddy G. N. and Prasad M.N.V., 1990 : Heavy Metal-binding Protein/ Peptides Occurance, Structure, Synthesis and Function: A Review Environ, Exp. Bot. 30: 251-264.

Venugopal B. and Lucky J.D., 1978: Chemical Toxicity of Metals and Metalloids. In Metal Toxicity in Mammals. B. Venugopal and J.D. Luckey, (Eds.) Vol. 2., pp. 76-86 Planum, New York/London.

Volkin E. and W.E. Cohn, 1954 : Methods Biochem. Anal. 1 : 287

Yannai S. and Berdicevsky I, 1995 : Formation of Organic Cadmium by Marine Microorganisms Eco-Toxicology and Environmental Safety. 32: 209-214.

9

BIODIVERSITY IN 21ST CENTURY
A STUDY OF WILDLIFE SANCTUARY OF ORISSA

R.L. Panigrahy*

Introduction

Biodiversity is a dynamic combination of genes, species and ecosystems existing on earth at any point of time since climatic change, depletion of ozone layer and biodiversity loss as well as sustainable ocean management are the global issues, it is obviously happened due to heavy industrialisation. Due to its cause and effect forests are disappearing at an alarming rate of about 16 million hectares per year. Burning of forest accounts for 20 per cent of carbon emission. Forest of India occupy an area about 75 million hectares *i.e.,* 22 per cent of land area with a varied species. 100 million people live in and around forests. Nature has endowed India with a large variety of plants *i.e.,* about 45000 species in number. The prolonged dry spell and the history of forests fires were clear warnings. So, preventive measures to stop the forest fires should include controlling of burning by creating firelines and maintaining constant vigil to prevent it from spreading.

Biodiversity by Human Activities

Human activities are constantly invading or threatening a new area of land and competing with the natural habitats of the various species on the planet. Human economic activities in 20th century have increasingly deleted the earths costal and marine resources. Approaching the 21st century, the biodiversity challenge remains the same. In the battle for protection and preservation of environment, there will not be a victor and a vanquished.

Biodiversity in India

India has a wide network of 75 national parks and 421 wildlife sactuaries. Botanical gardens should be properly managed for strengthening their existing facilities for conservation propagation of threatened endemic plant species and wildlife sanctuaries for animal and plant species and genes.

The future of the world is future of our children. Otherwise, children cannot name birds, insects, plants, herbs, fishes. One can not love what one does not know and they cannot know the natural environment they live in.

India has a rich resource of flora and fauna which is exitened day-by-day. It had 45,000 types of trees, 750 crore hectares of land are forest which is 22 per cent of the India's land area. The trees are the medicinal plants. Every plant has medicinal value. By which the great godly saints Charaka, Susruta, Dhanwantari and other saints of Himalayas and the Baidyas of local community are prayed everyday for their finding of natural medicines which is called as Ayurved. It is a veda which increases age of human being with clearing the diseases from body. Out of 600 types of rare medicinal plants, 60 are extincted from earth, 170 are going to be extincted. in 50 years back in 190 years of duration extinction rate is one species, now it happens in a duration of 50 years. In forest in a duration of 100 years, 3 sq. inch earth created, but now in a duration of 1000 years 1 sq. inch earth creating which also erases by rainwater. Heavy soil erosion is also became an alarming danger. Hence, every year in any time disaster arises.

Wildlife Sanctuaries of Orissa

Orissa is a land of vast, thick forests which cover almost 55,000 sq.m of land. The diversified ecological riches and environmental situation provide with excellent habitat for a very rich and diversified fauna. Wildlife is also very rich here. Orissa has around 13 wildlife sanctuaries. These sanctuaries and wildlife parks are a great sources of attraction for the tourists.

Nandankanan Sanctuary

Amidst the lush green Chandaka forest along the banks of the Kanjia lake lies Nandankanan, a beautiful park that got its name from "Nandan Van" meaning the Garden of the Heaven. This famous zoological park which is at a distance of

20 kms from Bhubaneswar, was established in the year 1960 and has been declared as a sanctuary in the year 1979. The main attractions of this sanctuary is the white tiger safari, the first of its kind in the world, spread over an area of 12 hectares, a lion safari of 20 hectares and a natural trail of 37 hectares, the Botanical Garden which has many rare and endangered species of flora from different parts of the world, the 620 metre long Ropeway that transports the visitors across the lake to view the Botanical Garden, Boating facility in the Kanjia lake, Toy Train running on a circular track along the lake and the thickly vegetated tract, a Reptile Park and a Bird Sanctuary. It has worlds largest collection of white tigers and has an international reputation for successfully breeding black panthers, gharial crocodiles and white tigers, Asiatic Lion Sangai, Nilgiri Langur, Indian Penguin, Mouse Deer and many land and water birds. One can take the opportunity to behold the kingly lions, clouded leopards, European Bears, Himalayan Black Bear, Rosy Pelican, Grey Pelican, Indian Python, King Cobra, exquisite collection of birds, etc. in the Zoo. The zoo has also given a new lease of life to one of the rarest creatures of the world—the white Kanan. The Acquaria homes to a large variety of freshwater fish, a number of species of crocodiles, lizards, turtles and snakes .

Buses are specially designed for taking people inside the Lion Safari, to facilitate them to see tigers and lions in natural habitat.

The Botanical Garden, which is famous all over for its unique collection of Cactus lies close to the Nandankanan. This garden also contains plants of different types like crotons, roses, etc. There is a ropeway connecting the Zoo with the Botanical garden. It is an ideal place for picnic.

Khalasuni Sanctuary

Khalasuni wildlife sanctuary is located in the Rairakhol sub-division of Sambalpur district. It is at a distance of 50 kms from Sambalpur. It covers an area of 116 sq.kms. The Tiger, leopard, elephant, bison, samber, spotted deer, barking deer, mouse deer, wilddogs, rare varieties of birds and reptiles attract the tourists.

Debrigarh Sanctuary

With an area of 346.91 sq.kms. the Debrigarh wildlife sanctuary is located in the Baragarh district. One can track important fauna like tiger, leopard, hyena, bison, samber, spotted deer, chousingha, resident and migratory birds, monitor lizard, chameleon etc. in this sanctuary.

Lakhari Valley Sanctuary

Located in Ganjam, it has a huge concentration of elephants and other wildlife.Blackbucks abound in then Bhetnai region.

Karlapat

About 35 km from Bhabanipatna, the district headquaters of Kalahandi, on Bhabanipatna-Thuamula-Rampur road is Karlapat famous for charming wildlife. Tigers, sambers, leopards, gaur and chitals have rich presence in these forest tracts.

Ushakothi Sanctuary

This is situated 22 kms from Sambalpur. It covers a forest area of about 285 square kms and the Hirakud Dam lies to its west. One can see elephants, tigers, panthers, sambers etc from strategically placed watch towers or from on boarding a jeep. The main attractions of this sanctuary are the rocket tail dragons and flying squirrels.

Bhitarakanika Sanctuary

It is called 'a slice of paradise on the earth and is one of the best sanctuaries in India .It is situated in the second largest mangrove forest in the country and provides an ideal habitat for reptiles including crocodiles, sea turtles and water monitor Lizards. This sanctuary which is located slightly away from the Gahirmatha Sanctuary, has protected the estuarine crocodile and its habitat since 1975.

This is located at the top of green delta formed by Mahanadi, Bramhani and Baitarani rivers. The picturesque location of this sanctuary, its mangrove forest, numerous varieties of wildlife particularly crocodiles in water, herds of deer on the bank and migrating birds on the sky is really a place of attraction. It has not only the world's biggest salt water crocodiles but also white crocodiles. The mangrove supports a large variety of bird life such as storks, egrets, white ibis, six pieces of kingfishers, as well as migratory ducks from Siberia and Hungary. This sanctuary can be visited by special permission in order to maintain the ecosystem of the place.

Kuldiha Sanctuary

The Kuldiha wildlife sanctuary is located in the district of Balasore with an area of 272.75 sq.kms. This sanctuary is linked to the Similipal National Park through Sukhupata hills and Nato hill ranges. One can feel the wildlife of elephants, bison, samber, giant squirrel, leopard, varieties of birds like hill myna, peacock, hornbills and varieties of reptiles here.

Ambapani Sanctuary

The picturesque Ambapani hills present a panoramic view of nature. It is located 77 kms from Bhawanipatna . It is particularly famous for the deity of Budharaja in a small temple at the foot of a hill. A frolicking valley known by Haldigundi in this range of hills exhibits some peculiar features due to the reflected rays of the sun. This sanctuary inhabits black panthers, samber and spotted deer.

Chilika Lake

The Chilika Lake is a sanctuary and winter resort for migratory birds, some coming from as far as Siberia.Nestling in the heart of coastal Orissa, Chilika is India's biggest inland lake. Spread over 1,100 square kilometers, stretching across the length of the three districts of Puri, Khurda and Ganjam, it joins up with the Bay of Bengal through a narrow mouth, forming an enormous lagoon of brackish water. Dotted with many emerald green islands with colourful names such as Honeymoon Island and Breakfast Island, Chilka is home to a rich variety of aquatic fauna.

Encircled by hills all along its arched shape, Chilika lake's colour changes with passing clouds overhead and the shifting sun . The water ripples languidly, occasionally rippling with a gentle breeze across from the Bay of Bengal.

Containing a large variety of fish, the lake provides a livelihood to thousands of fishermen. Hundreds of boats sail out daily on the lake's blue expanse in search of sight providing an insight into the pageant of rural India at its colourful best .

Simlipal Tiger Reserves

This is one of the National parks of India situated in Mayurbhanj district in Orissa.It is spread over an area of 2,750 sq.kms and was chosen by the Project Tiger for conserving the country's depleting tiger population. This park has within its boundaries about 95 Royal Bengal Tigers, leopards, elephants, muggar crocodiles and a number of reptiles and 231 species of birds.

The vast expanse and changing topography as well as the vegetational and climatic variations in Simlipal have been the major reasons for the successful breeding of the flora and fauna. The varied beauty of the lush green forests, mountains and valleys give an extravagant view. Jashipur, one of the two entry points to the park, has a crocodile sanctuary; the other entry point being Lulung.

The best way to see as much as possible would be to take a package tour which would take in the Barehipani waterfall (399 meters) and the Joranda waterfall (150 meters), the lush grasslands of Bachhuri Chara, the Meghasani peak(1,158 meters) and the wildlife in the environs.

Gahirmatha Turtle Sanctuary

This is a stretch of beach that is used for breeding the giant Olive Turtles, who travel all the way from Pacific Ocean to mate and lay their eggs. Every year, thousands of wondrous creatures are seen here. The Government of Orissa has made special arrangements in order to protect the turtles. This is also the harbouring ground for various kinds of migratory birds.

Baisipalli Sanctuary

Baisipalli wildlife sanctuary was established in 1981 in the eastern ghats and rises from almost sea level to about 900 metres. It is situated at a distance of 60 kilometeres from Nayagarh and extends over 168.35 square kilometres. Apart from elephants and tigers there are also samber, mouse deer and a fascinating variety of fauna including migrating and resident avifauna.

Satakoshia George Sanctuary

This sanctuary was established in 1976 and the total sanctuary area is about 745.52 sq.kms. This sanctuary is at a distance of 58 kms from Angul. About 10 kms to the south of the george at Purnakote and Labangi, Gharials have made their home in the Mahanadi river and this sanctuary was established primarily to protect these crocodiles, an endangered species.

Chandaka Elephant Sanctuary

The Chandaka elephant sanctuary, the first of its kind in India, was established in 1982 with a view to promote eco-regeneration of depleting environment. About 20 kms away from Bhubaneswar, it is a dense forest covering 190 sq. kms. where around 100 elephant roam freely. There are a number of watch towers set for the visitors to watch these huge animals.

Hadgarh Sanctuary

Hadgarh wildlife sanctuary is located in the district of Keonjhar only at a distance of 20 kms from Bhadrak on NH-5. It was established in the year 1978 covering an area of about 191.06 sq. kms. Amidst the dense Sal forest there are leopards, wilddogs and elephants etc. The dam here is an ideal habitat for the muggar crocodiles.

Kotagad Sanctuary

Kotagad wildlife sanctuary is situated in the Baliguda sub-division og Kandhamal district covering an area of 399.05 sq. kms. One can see here the important species that include tigers, leopards, bisons, elephants, samber, spotted deer, varieties of birds(peacock, red jungle fowl etc.) and reptiles.

Reference

1. Orissa Government website : www.orissagov.nic.in

10

HEAVY METAL POLLUTION IN WATER
DEVILS IN DISGUISE

K.L. Jain*

Water is indispensable for life and it is worst affected by various anthropogenic activities. Distribution of water resources on this planet is uneven. Thirty per cent of the global water is found as inland water, while 70 per cent is present in oceans. Almost seventy five per cent of this inland water found on the surface of earth is locked in glaciers and icebergs. The total area of freshwater resources covers only two million sq. kms. Though water is a renewable resource yet contamination of water by undesirable substances is creating a serious havoc. The stresses exerted by the industrial developmental processes culminate in the mortality of fish and fish food organisms. The instances of destruction of breeding grounds and impediments in migration are well documented (Jhingran, 1991). Although, water is a renewable resource, yet the contamination of water by undesirable substances flowing in through the industrial effluents and the city sewage systems is creating a serious problem these days. Various toxic chemicals added in water being non-biodegradable, they accumulate in these sources.

Fisheries are one of the most rewarding activities now a day particularly in the developing countries, including India. Being a potential source of protein rich animal food as well as livelihood for human beings, fish constitutes one of the major components of global model of world food production. Global fisheries, however, is facing a constant decline in fish stocks, both in coastal and inland water resources on account of continuously increasing water pollution. Large amount of organic and inorganic wastes are discharged into water bodies by agricultural, industrial and the domestic activities. It

* **Department of Zoology and Aquaculture, Haryana Agricultural University, Hissar-125004, Haryana, India.**

includes acids, pesticides, detergents and the heavy metals. These effluents are being indiscriminately thrown into the natural water bodies and the level of wastes exceeds the self purifying capacity of the water bodies. This results in drastic changes in the physico-chemical and the biological characteristics of water bodies. These water bodies thus become almost unfavourable for health, survival, growth and reproduction of aquatic fauna including fish.

Industrial development is the compelling need of increasing world population. Almost all the major industries contribute to the water pollution. Many workers till date have reported physico-chemical status of industrial effluents and of river water receiving the wastes (Kumar, 2002). As per an estimate about 50 per cent of the existing species of flora and fauna may disappear in the next few decades if the environmental pollution continued increasing at the same rate. The need of the hour is to rationalise the use of industrial effluents, *vis-a-vis* to minimise their interference with the biotic components including fishes.

The heavy metal pollution is worst in natural waters. These are known as 'Devils in disguise' due to their lipophilic nature and bio-accumulation in animal tissues. Notwithstanding, their persistence and non-degradation in soil and water systems, the economic reasons compel us to keep them using. Almost all the major rivers and lakes throughout the world today are known to be heavily polluted with heavy metals and other toxic chemicals (Jain and Mittal, 2004). Heavy metals affect various physiological, histological and biochemical functions of fish (Jain and Sharma, 2003). Heavy metals include all the metals with atomic weight above sodium. The major heavy metals adversely influencing the body functions are cadmium (Cd), lead (Pb), chromium (Cr), mercury (Hg), arsenic (As), nickel (Ni) and cobalt (Co). Mukhopadhyay *et al.*, (1994) have studied the overall impact of pollution stress on aquatic organisms *viz.* fish, planktons and zoo benthos. He concluded that heavy metals form an important group of pollutants which play an adverse role on the productive potentiality of an ecosystem particularly in the industrial zone. The toxicity of these metals depends upon their chemical form, interaction with each other and the various hydro-biological parameters. The interaction among various chemical pollutants in the aquatic ecosystem may further be synergistic, antagonistic or additive. In synergism, toxicological manifestations of the individual chemicals when in combination often get increased. Kaviraj and Konar (1983) determined the LC50 and LC95 values of Hg and Cd mixture for the fish *T. mossambicus* which was in the range of 90.0 to 190.5 ppm while Sehgal and Saxena (1986) examined the acute toxicity of Cd and Zn to *Puntius ticto*. They reported the LC50 for 24, 48, 72 and 96 h as 35, 30, 28 and 26 ppm for Cd and 75, 70, 66 and 60 ppm for Zn respectively. Due to their adverse effects on the aquatic ecosystems, it is important to identify the sources of the discharge of heavy metals into systems nationwide (Biney *et al.*, 1994) and appropriate measures to control them. It is thus also important to monitor the bio-accumulation of these metals in a system, in order to assess its impact on human health and the health of the organism.

As pollutants the heavy metals were first identified about four decades ago in Japan with the identification of a disease Minamata, due to Hg toxicity in fishes (Takeuchi, 1968). The heavy metals are known not only to cause physiological disorders (Heath, 1995), their accumulation in fish tissue may further deteriorate the quality of fish flesh. This article is thus a resume of some important biochemical aspects of heavy metal toxicity in fish in an attempt to educate people about the impelling dangers of heavy metal hazards to fisheries and the humans as the fish consumers.

These heavy metals even when present in trace amounts can cause abnormalities in fish physiology, morphology as well as behaviour. Pandey *et al.* (2004) estimated varying concentrations of heavy metals *i.e.* Ni (0.06-0.08 mg/l), Zn (0.02-0.8 mg/l), Ca (nil-0.70 mg/l), Pb (nil-0.26 mg/l), Cd (nil-0.84 mg/l) As (nil-0.16 mg/l) in the different parts of the river Pandu at Kanpur. Kaviraj (1989) made a survey of Hooghly estuary during 1977-81 and reported 112.2 ppm Zn, 10 ppm Cu and 0.3 ppm Cr in Shrimps.

Saikia *et al.* (1988) studied the water and the wet sediments of the river Ganga for a stretch of 480 kms extending from Badrinath to Narora and reported the presence of Mn, Fe, Co,

Cu and Zn below the toxic limits thereby indicating the water to be unpolluted. The lower stretch of the river is free from any anthropogenic activities which contribute to heavy metal pollution, hence they attribute to the occurrence of metals in very small amounts to the geo-chemical source.

Bhagwant (2003) determined the concentrations of Cu and Fe in the tissues and the organs of four edible fish species from the Bay of Pourdre D' by flame atomic absorption spectrophotometer. The extent of accumulation of the metal vary which may possibly be due to the differences in the behaviour and the feeding habits of the fish species. Zhou *et al.* (2003) demonstrated that the accumulation of Cu in the tissues of fish was related to the metallic species (Zn, Pb or Cd), concentration of metals and the type of tissue. The interactions become more significant with an increase in the concentration of metals on account of biological magnification. The accumulation of the Cu is said to decrease in the gills in an interaction of a combination of metals, but increased in the liver and brain. The metal mixture could not affect the muscle for accumulation of Cu. The order of Cu accumulation in the tissues of the fish was liver>gill>brain>muscles and the other metals did not change this order of Cu accumulation in the tissues.

The concentration of the different heavy metals *i.e.,* As, Se, Cd, Co, Fe, Cu, Mn, Ni, Mb, Zn and Pb in the different fish species range from 0.004-80.36 μg/kg body weight of the fish having the maximum concentration of Zn. Total Hg was found to be high *i.e.,* 0.61 μg/g. 12 out of 17 fishes exceeded the safe level of 0.01 mg/kg of different heavy metals (Gutleb *et al.,* 2002). Bonnel *et al.* (1960) observed that Cd is deposited initially both in the liver and kidney in comparable concentration while on prolonged exposure, it accumulates preferentially in the kidney of the fish. The kidneys did not accumulate As as in the liver. The gills did not seem to accumulate any substantial amount of As during continued exposure. This observation might be due to the fast elimination of As via the gills. In another study various organs of the common carp, *C. carpio* were analysed for the heavy metals. Significantly higher Hg contents were detected in the muscle,

Cd and Zn in the kidney and Cu in the liver. A significantly higher contents of Cu and Zn was found in eggs also (Svobodova *et al.*, 2002).

Sultana and Rao (1998) studied the bio-accumulation pattern of the Zn, Cu, Pb and the Cdin grey mullet, M. cephalus of harbour waters of Vishakhapatnam, India. They reported that the alimentary canal and the gills can be considered as the interface of the organism and its ambience.. Alimentary canal is also known for its excretory functions for some metals like Zn...Deb and Santra (1997) analysed the bio-accumulation of Cu, Pb, Zn and Cr in the liver, intestine, muscle and the brain in four fishes, *C. punctatus, T. mossambica, C. catla* and *L. rohita* in a sewage fed jheel ecosystem. There has been some evidence of metal excretion in fish also when returned to normal water, as indicated by the decreasing order in the Cd accumulation in tissues of the 8 weeks old common carp C. carpio and the order was found to be gut > kidney > liver = gill > muscle. Whereas in the contaminated water Kraal *et al.* (1995) reported the corresponding values in the decreasing order i.e. gut > gills > kidney > liver > muscle. Since, the concentrations of the metals found in tissues of these fishes reflect the external concentrations; they become ideal tools for monitoring environmental levels.

While considering the action of the toxic chemicals in fish the liver is of key importance. It is the primary organ of bio-transformation of the organic xenobiotics, and probably also for the excretion of the harmful trace metals. Since many of these metals and the organic tend to accumulate in high concentrations in the liver, therefore the cells in liver are exposed to a very high (often several orders of magnitude) levels of these harmful chemicals as compared to those present in the environment or in other organs of the fish. The liver serves a number of functions related to other physiological activities such as interconversion of the foodstuff and the metabolism of these hormones. The potential effects of the xenobiotics on the liver are numerous, but are often seen indirectly.

The test fishes exposed to the heavy metals at a sub lethal dose level in general show reduced growth and a decline in the energy yielding chemical components particularly the glycogen. A great amount of carbohydrates is stored in the liver as glycogen. Though glycogen stored in muscles of a fish are an important store but the concentration found in the liver are far more. The glycogen appears to be utilised to counteract the toxicity stress and ultimately influencing the growth rates. There are many such studies indicating a significant decline in the glycogen in the liver or in the muscles (Shelly *et al.*, 2006). An exposure to the metal possibly stimulates the hormones which accelerate the glycogen breakdown or inhibition of those chemicals involved in the synthesis of glycogen.

Liver glycogen depletion is said to be maximum with Co as well as Cd, followed by Ni and the least with Zn. Whereas, the muscle glycogen depletion was found to be in the order: Cd > Co > Ni > Zn (Shelly, 2006). Similar results were reported in *C.carpio* (Cicik and Engin, 2005), where the glycogen levels in the liver and muscle tissues of the fish exposed to predetermined concentrations of Cd (0.05, 0.1,0.5,1 mg/l) were significantly lowered by 23.72 per cent and 29.05 per cent respectively as compared to the control fish. A dose dependent increase in the glycogen phosphorylase and a dose dependent decrease in glycogen synthetase were also observed by Hontella *et al* (1996), thereby suggesting an increased glycogenolytic potential in the liver of salmon exposed to Cd. An increase in the phosphofructo-1-kinase activity was also observed after a Cd 8-hr exposure that resulted in a stress leading to increased glycogenolysis.

A prolonged environmental stress in the fish makes the adaptation difficult and creates a weakness in the fish. This weekness is characterised by a decrease in the liver glycogen and the serum cortisol levels, which subsequently create alterations in the metabolism and also shortens the lifespan of the organisms (Heath, 1995). Cd was reported to decrease the glycogen reserves in *H. fossilis* by stimulating the glycolytic enzymes like lactate dehydrogenase, pyruvate dehydrogenase and succinate dehydrogenase (Sastry and Subhadra, 1982).

Gill and Pant (1981) reported that juveniles and the adults of *Puntius conchonius* when exposed to Hg in soft and hard waters, to 36.3 and 60.5 μg $HgCl_2$/l, there was hyperglycemia persisting up to four weeks. The glycogen levels in liver and brain remained low up to three weeks but an increase in myocardium glycogen was registered after an exposure of 8 weeks demonstrating simultaneous changes in the blood *i.e.* erythropenia. A fall in the hemoglobin after exposure of 1-3 week and polycythemia after an exposure of 6-8 weeks was recorded.

Toxicity of heavy metals is enhanced in combination. This was indicated by an increased toxicity of Cd in combination with Zn (Shelly, 2006). James *et al.,* (1991) made a similar observation and observed reduction in the liver carbohydrate content in fishes exposed to Cd and Cu+Cd, which was about 32 and 63 per cent, respectively as compared to control. An insignificant change in the liver carbohydrate content was observed in the animals treated with Cu alone. Cu in combination with either Zn or Cd adversely affected the liver carbohydrate content which was reduced by 54 per cent and 63 per cent fn the fish reared in Cu+Zn and Cu+Cd combinations, respectively.

Khanna and Gill (1975) suggested the possibility of an imbalance in the pancreatic hormones involved in the carbohydrate metabolism, due to damage of pancreas by the toxic substances. In *C. punctatus* administration of cobalt chloride and cobalt nitrate induced hyperglycemia along with the degranulation and vacuolisation of the pancreatic tissue in the initial stages while a damage of the α-cells in the later stages.

Reduction in protein contents is another parameter indicating metal toxicity effects in fish. The fish stops feeding in the toxicant rich medium. The stress and starvation may also result in the break down of the body protein to provide energy (proteolysis), causing thus a reduction in the total body protein level in the fish. Another reason for the depletion in the protein content in the body of the fish may be lesser protein synthesis or it may also be due to the utilisation of amino acids in other catabolic reactions.

The effects of Ni, Co, Cd and Zn independently and also in combination were studied to estimate changes in the crude protein levels (mg/g) in the total tissue and the muscles of fishes exposed to the metals (Shelly, 2006). This data clearly revealed that when the concentration of the metals was increased, the protein levels became lowered as compared to that of the control. The maximum reduction was observed in the treatments of a combination of Cd and Zn as well as that of Cd alone.

A decrease in the crude protein content in the fish *C. carpio* exposed to 0, 0.8, 4 and 20mμM Cd was observed by Hans and Ronny (2001). They observed an increased activity of aspartate aminotransferase and alanine aminotransferase, thereby suggesting that proteolysis is intended to increase the role of proteins in the energy production during Cd stress. The effects of Cd toxicity on the biochemical, enzymatic and haematological parameters were studied by Dinodia (2001) in the fresh water fish species *L. rohita, C. mrigala* and *C. carpio.* Maximum decline in the carbohydrate content reported was 19.2, 42.46 and 38.3 per cent respectively in *L. rohita, C. mrigala* and *C. carpio.* Decline in protein content was 21.3 to 25.5 per cent and that in liver glycogen was from 11.2 to 45.2 per cent There are also some reports about remediation of metal toxicity in fish. Ahilan and Jeyaseelan (2001) studied the effect of vitamin B_{12} and $CoCl_2$ on the growth and maturation of goldfish. $CoCl_2$ incorporated at 7.5 ppm gave positive results for both the gonadal development and the growth. Among the doses tested for vitamin B_{12}, the 25 ppm concentration had shown the highest response for both *i.e.,* maturation as well as growth. Sen and Chatterjee (1979) reported that an exposure of the fish *C. carpio* to $CoCl_2$ and B-Complex resulted in an increase in the protein content. It was attributed to enhanced growth of carps as a result of the effects of $CoCl_2$ and B-Complex.

A low molecular weight cytosolic protein metallothionin (MT) possess an inherent capacity to bind differentially with metals like Pb, Cd, Cr, Ni and As in various fishes. The accumulation of metals in various intracellular compartments is thus a function of relative rates of the metal binding and release as determined by their relative metal binding affinity and competition among different metals for binding to MT. The latter is a protective protein responsible for elimination of toxic metals. Generally liver, kidney, gills and the intestine are the main sites for MT synthesis in fishes which is either stored or excreted. An exposure of the animals to the specific metals and the ions induces the synthesis of MT and they preferentially bind these toxic metals making them harmless and thus yielding metal scavenging effect (Rema and Philip, 1996). The reduction is up to the extent to which the essential metabolic activities would otherwise be inhibited. It explains the development of tolerance by the animal to the transition metallothionin. When the concentration increases and overcomes the capacity of this natural detoxifying system, various adverse effects which are proportional to the metal dose level are observed.. The Cd has been reported to stimulate MT formation even at very low dose levels but its chronic exposure reduces its binding capacity and as the fishes were exposed metal free water, the recovery occurred but not completely changes in the blood parameters like blood cholesterol level, RBC count, haemoglobin content and the haematocrit (HCt) per cent in the fishes exposed to the different dose levels of different heavy metals is a clear indication of their toxicity. A significant decrease in the blood cholesterol levels, RBC count and the haematocrit per cent as a result of heavy metal toxicity have been observed in fishes (Shelly, 2006). The winter flounder and striped bass exhibited a distinct anaemia when exposed to Hg (inorganic) for 60 days (Dawson, 1982). The magnitude of the change was smaller in the flounder even though a higher Hg concentration was used with the species. Anaemia has also been reported with a higher and shorter duration exposures.

Heavy metal toxicity whether individual or in the combination have been reported to cause a significant decline in the blood cholesterol levels (Ferrando and Moliner, 1991). It is presumed that the reduction in circulating cholesterol level in the blood is either due to its more utilisation during corticosteroidogenesis, as it is precursor for steroid hormones, or depressed de novo synthesis. Methylmercury has also been reported to decrease the serum cholesterol in Bluegill fish, *Lepomis macrochirus* (Dutta and Haghighi, 1986).

The toxicity of lead influences mainly the blood parameters such as RBC counts, Hb contents, HCt and the oxygen carrying capacity. James *et al.,* (1993) exposed *O. mossambicus* to sublethal concentration of Pb and observed a dose dependent decrease in RBC count and Hb, thereby leading to anaemia. It may be due to the inhibition of erythropoesis and the hemosynthesis. The test animals after exposured to lead toxicity when transferred to Pb free water improved the status of haematological parameters and normal state was found to be restored in 45-65 days, depending upon the Pb dose level. Cd cause a maximum reduction in all the blood parameters as reported by earlier workers also. Cd has been reported to cause anaemia in different fish species at a lower as well as higher concentrations (Gill and Pant, 1985; Houston *et al.*, 1993). Cd also causes an abnormally large number of malformed erythrocytes (Houston *et al.*, 1993) which implies a lesion in the machinery for forming blood cells. Measurements of the enzyme delta-aminolevulinic acid dehydrase (ALA-D) in the kidney have shown a compensatory increase as a result of exposure of Cd (Johansson-Sjobeck and Larsson, 1978). This indicates that the initial steps of the synthesis of Hb are not blocked by Cd, rather in spite of the increased enzyme activity, Hb synthesis still goes down. The net effect is a slowing down of erythrocyte maturation (Houston *et al.*, 1993). In addition to the reduction in the capacity to produce normal blood cells, some workers have also noted increased rates of erythrocyte breakdown.

Chronic exposure to metals commonly cause sever damage to some vital body organs like skin, gills, liver, intestine, kidneys and brain. Most common features are cell prolification, necrosis and vaccuolation. It also caused breakage of the villi of intestine, cell swellings, shrinkage of kidney glomeruli and the degeneration of goblet cells (Gupta *et al.*, 2004).

Great deals of changes induced by the heavy metals are also reported in the skin of the fish. Sloughing of the epidermis and a few regions of the dermis could be seen in the skin of most of the metal treated fishes. The concentrations of Ni, Co, Cr and Pb in the skin tissues of the fish *Lethrinus lentjan* collected from the coastal waters of the United Arab Emirates between May and June 1993 (El-Shahawi and Al-Yousuf, 1998) were recorded. The concentrations of the metals in the skin samples decreased in the following order: Cr > Pb > Ni > Co. The reported accumulation of these metals in the tissues could possibly be responsible for the degenerative changes. Skin neoplasm occurred among salmon in a number of Russian fish farms during the past 2-3 years.

The upper layers of the skin in a fish serve to secrete the mucous which serves an important function of protecting the integument from desiccation by binding a large amount of water and also help in keeping the skin clear for respiration by precipitating mud held in suspension in water (Munshi and Hughes, 1992). Metal concentrations in skin samples decreased in the following order: Cr>Pb>Ni>Co. The accumulation of these metals in the tissues as has been reported could possibly be responsible for the degenerative changes. The erosion of the outer epithelial layer and the middle layer of the epidermis which is rich in mucous secreting cells might cause hindrance or impairment in protective and respiratory functions of the skin. The concentrations of the chromatophores was revealed in the metal exposed fish which may be related to depigmentation of the integument on a prolonged exposure to the heavy metals. Fusion of the gill lamellae and lifting of gill epithelium from the supporting elements are such effects which reduce the surface areas available for gaseous and other exchange and lengthen the distance over which the exchange diffusion occurs.

The mechanism of action of the heavy metals in relation to their toxic impact on the gonads of the fish is not well known and requires further investigations. However, various workers have attempted to describe different mechanisms of action. Kumar and Pant (1981) have attributed a direct effect of heavy metals on the fish gonads, besides their possible action through pituitary. Ram and Sathyanesan (1983) suggested inhibition of the action of pituitary gonadotrophs and somatotrophs in *C. punctatus* exposed to Hg.

Sharma (2003) studied the effects of Hg, Co and endosulfan alone and Hg in combination with Co and endosulfan on the morphological, biochemical and histopathological changes in the fresh water fish species, *C. mrigala.* She observed severe morphological aberrations like fin erosion, descaling, haemorrhage, protruding eyes etc. Carbohydrate, protein and liver glycogen level were reduced by 8.61, 7.09 and 8.10 per cent respectively due to Co toxicity; by 12.84, 13.02 and 13.57 per cent, respectively due to Hg toxicity; by 35.73, 25.52 and 27.27 per cent respectively due to Hg+Co treatment and maximum reduction of 40.15, 30.13 and 45.25 per cent respectively due to endosulfan+Hg treatment. Thus, it was observed that though mercury being a toxic metal induces large number of morphological, biochemical and histopathological changes in the fish, however its effects were further enhanced in combination with Co as well as endosulfan.

Mittal (2005) studied the effects of toxic heavy metals As, Hg, Co and Ni alone and in combination (As+Hg, As+Co, As+Ni) on fresh water fish species *C. mrigala.* Significant alterations in biochemical parameters (carbohydrate, protein and liver glycogen level) as well as histology (of gills, liver and intestine) were observed. Maximum reduction in the carbohydrate, protein and liver glycogen level *i.e.,* 33.5, 29.5 and 40.0 per cent respectively was due to As+Hg treatment. Severe histopathological aberrations like degeneration and fusion of secondary gill lamellae, heterogenous distribution of hepatocytes, rupturing and vacuolation in intestinal mucosa were also observed as a result of heavy metal toxicity. The most toxic metal reported was As and further its toxic effects were enhanced in the presence of other metals.

Abhas *et al.* (2003) studied that Cu and Pb are among the most widely distributed common pollutants in the aquatic environment. The 96h LC_{50} also bioassays were carried out so as to determine the toxicity of these two heavy metals (Cu and Pb) in the blue Tilapia, *Oreochromis aureus.* The 96 h LC_{50} of Cu and the Pb were found to be 8.17 and 25.86 mg/l, respectively. Groups of the adult and healthy *O. aureus* were subjected to the acute (lethal) concentration (96 LC_{50}) of each above metal and examined after 24 and 96 hours. Other groups were subjected to the chronic (sublethal) concentration (1/10 LC_{50}) of each metal and examined after 6 and 12 weeks. The lethal and the sublethal concentrations of Cu and Pb altered the behavioural activities of the treated fish. The gills, liver, kidney and the spleen tissues were irritated and injured thereby causing dysfunction in these organs. Haemoglobin contents increased in the fish toxicated by Cu and decreased in those toxicated by Pb. Serum glucose increased in all the groups treated with Cu or Pb. Moreover, the creatinine and the uric acid levels were also elevated.

Bonnell *et al.,* (1960) observed that Cd is deposited initially both in the liver and kidney in comparable concentration while on prolonged exposure, it accumulates preferentially in the kidney of the fish. The kidneys did not accumulate as much As as the liver. The gills did not seem to accumulate any substantial amount of As during continued exposure. This observation might be due to the fast elimination of As via the gills.

Metals may act synergistically where the toxic response is greater than the sum of individual toxicities. James *et al.* (1992) studied the effects of sublethal doses of (Cu, Cd, Zn) and their mixtures on the activities of key respiratory enzymes, succinate dehydrogenase, (SDH) and glyceraldehyde dehydrogenase (GDH) and their recovery following the withdrawal of treatments in the freshwater fish *O. mossambicus.* On the basis of 96 h LC_{50}, Cu was highly toxic followed by Zn and Cd. In combination, (Cu + Zn + Cd) was extremely toxic than any other combinations and the Zn + Cd combination was least toxic. A significant gradual decrease in SDH with a concomitant inerease in GDH activity in liver, brain, muscle and the gill of animals exposed to metal suggest a metabolic shift from the aerobiosis to anaerobiosis. Exposed individuals when transferred to the metal impoverished water showed an improvement in SDH activity and a decline in GDH activity thereby suggesting a slow reversal to aerobic metabolism. *O. mossambicus* needs more time for complete recovery.

Dinodia *et al.*. (2003) studied the effects of Cd toxicity on proteolytic enzyme activity in some freshwater carps and it was found that proteolytic enzyme activity declined maximally in *C. mrigala* from 26 per cent at 2.5 ppm to 55.6 per cent at 5.0 ppm. In *L. rohita* it showed maximum decline at 5.0 ppm (32.6%) as compared to the control fish., Hyperplasia and fusion of secondary lamellae of the fish causing a failure of the respiratory mechanism James *et al.* (1991b) studied the individual as well as the combined effects of Zn, Cu and Cd on the growth of *O. mossambicus.* The combined effect of metals on the food utilisation in *O. mossambicus* was more severe than when used individually. The reduction in the growth rate in animals exposed to Zn, Cd and Cu was about 32, 42 and 47 per cent respectively and in those exposed to metal in the combination of Zn + Cd, Cu + Zn and Cu + Cd, it was 65, 73 and 86 per cent, respectively as compared to the control. Animals exposed to the metals showed significant decline in the food intake. Metabolic rate increased by 34 and 70 per cent in the animals exposed to Cu and a combination of Cu and Cd. The combination of Zn + Cd was less toxic than the combinations of Cu + Zn and Cu + Cd on the food utilisation parameters. It was also concluded that the combinations of Cu + Zn and Cu + Cd were highly toxic because of their synergistic effect.

Lipid peroxidation is also important indicator, as it reveal free ion composition in tissues after metal toxity in fish. It is reduced in the liver tissues in the control fish. It increased with the increasing Cd concentration in water. It was concluded that Cd participates in the oxidation reactions in the liver cells to produce lipid peroxides. Chattarjee and Bhattacharya (1984) demonstrated in teleosts, pollutants influence thryoxine release mediated via the peroxidase system of iodination. Mixture of toxicants either prepared in the laboratory or collected from a factory discharge, are equally detrimental towards the thyroxine homoeostasis. Inhibition of head kidney peroxidase was usually associated with a decrease in iodide peroxidase activity and blood thyroxine level.

The above stated profile of various biochemical and functional changes in fishes following heavy metal exposure clearly suggest a serious concern for heavy metal water pollution in rivers or other water bodies in use for fish rearing and culture and finding ways for their remediation.

References

Abhas, H.H. Zaghloul, K.H. and Mousa. M.A. 2003. Effect of Some Heavy Metal Pollutants on Some Biochemical and Histopathological Changes in Blue Tilapia, Oreochromes Aureus. Egyptian J. Agric. Res. 80 (3): 1395-1410.

Ahilan, B. and Jeyaseelan, M.J. 2001. Effect of Cobalt Chloride and Vitamin B_{12} on the Growth and Gonadal Maturation of Goldfish *Carassius Auratus. Indian J.* Catfish, *Icatalurus Punctatus. Bull. Environ. Contam. Toxicol.* 44: 435.

Bhagwant, S. 2003. Lead, Copper and Zinc Levels in Organ Tissue Samples of Three Edible Lagoon Fish Species. 2003. *Poll. Res.* *22* (2):299-303.

Biney, C., Amazy, A.T., Calamari, D., Kaba, N., Mbome, I.L., Naeve, H., Ochumba, P.B.O., Osibanju, O., Radegonde, V. and Saad, M.A.H. 1994. Review of Heavy Metals in the African Aquatic Environment. *Ecotoxicol. Environ. Safety.* 31: 134-159.

Bonnel, J.A., Ross, J.H. and King, E. 1960. Renal Lesions in Experimental Cadmium Poisoning. *Dist. J. Indian Med.* 17 : 69-80.

Chatterjee, S. and Bhattacharya, S. 1984. Response of Climbing Perch, Anabas Testudineus to Industrial Pollutants: Head Kidney Peroxidase, Iodide Peroxidase and Blood Thyroxine Profiles. Water Air Soil Poll. 25 : 161-174.

Cicik, B and Engin, K. 2005. The Effects of Cd on Levels of Glucose in Serum and Glycogen Reserves in the Liver and Muscle Tissues of *Cyprinus Carpio* (L., 1758). *Tukrish. J. Anim.Sci.* 29:113-117.

Dawson, M.A. 1982. Effects of Long-term Mercury Exposure on Haematology of Striped Bass, *Morone Saxatilis. Fish. Bull.* 80: 389.

Deb, S.C. and Santra, S.C. 1997. Bioaccumulation of Metals in Fishes. An *in vivo* Experimental Study of Sewage Fed Ecosystem. *Journal Article ASEA*- Part-3.

Dinodia, G.S. 2001. Studies on the Effects of Cadmium Toxicity in Some Fresh Water Fishes. M.Sc. Thesis, Department of Zoology and Aquaculture, CCS HAU, Hisar.

Dinodia, G.S., Gupta, R.K., Jain, K.L. and Yadava, N.K. 2003. Cadmium Toxicity and Its Effect on the Proteolytic Enzyme Activity in Some Fresh Water Carps. Proceedings of 3rd Interaction Workshop, December 17-18, CCS HAU Hisar. pp. 195-199.

Dutta, H.M. and Haghighi, A.Z. 1986. Methylmercuric Chloride and Serum Cholesterol Level in Bluegill *(Lepomis Machrochirus). Bull. Environ. Contam. Toxicol.* 36 : 181-185.

El-Shahawi, M.S. and AI-Yousuf, M.H. 1998. Heavy Metal (Ni. Co, Cr and Pb) Contamination in Liver and Skin Tissues of *Lelhrinus Lentjan* Fish. Family: Lethrinidae (Teleost) from the Arabian Gulf. *Int. J. Food Sci. Nutr:* 49 (6): 447-451.

Ferrando, M.D. and Moliner, E.A. 1991. Effect of Lindane on Blood of a Freshwater Fish. *Bull. Environ. Contam. Toxicol.* 47:465-470.

Gill, T.S. and Pant, J.C. 1981. Effects of Sublethal Concentration of Mercury in a Teleost *Puntius Conchonius :* Biochemical and Haematological Responses. *Indian J. Expt. Biol.* 19:571-573.

Gill, T.S. and Pant, J.C. 1985. Erythrocytic and Leucocytic Response to Cd Poisoning in Freshwater Fish, *Puntius Conchonius*. *Environ. Res.* 36: 327 - 337.

Gupta, R.K., Jain. K.L.. Yadava, N.K. and Dharmendra Kumar. 2004. Lead Contamination in Aquatic Medium and Its Impact on Body Tissue Composition in Indian Major Carps. Proceedings of the National Workshop on Rational Use of Water Resources for Aquaculture. (CCS, Haryana Agricultural Univ. Hisar, March 18-19, 2004): pp. 208-210.

Gutleb, A.C. Helsberg, A and Mitchell, C. 2002. Heavy Metal Concentrations in Fish from a Pristine Rainforest Valley in Peru: A Baseline Study Before Starting of Oil Drilling Activities. *Bull. Environ. Contam. Toxicol.* 69 (4): 523-529.

Hans. De-Smet and Rony. B. 2001. Stress Responses and Changes in Protein Metabolism in Carp, *Cyprinus Carpio* During Cadmium Exposure. *Ecotoxicol Environ. Safely.*48 (3): 255-262.

Heath, A.G. 1995. Water Pollution and Fish Physiology. Second Ed. Lewis Publishers.

Houston, A., Blahut, S., Murad, A and Amikrtharaj, P. 1993. Changes in Erythron Organisation During Prolonged Cadmium Exposure: An Indicator of Heavy Metal Stress. *Can. J. Fish. Aquat. Sci.* 50:217.

Jain K.L. and Mittal, V. 2004. Heavy Metal Pollution in Surface Water Bodies and Its Impact on Fishes. Proceedings of the National Workshop on Rational Use of Water Resources for Aquaculture. (Hisar. March 18-19. 2004).

Jain, K.L. and Sharma. M. 2003. Toxic Effects of Mercury and Cobalt on Biochemical Composition of Freshwater Fish *Cirrhinus Mrigala*. Proceedings of 3rd Interaction Workshop, December 17-18, 2003. CCS HAU, Hisar. pp.203-207

James, R., Al-agurathinam, S. and Sampath, K. 1993. Haematological Changes and Oxygen Consumption in *Oreochromis Mossambicus* Exposed to Sublethal Concentrations of Lead. *Indian J. Fisheries.* 40(3): 193-196.

James, R., Sampath, K., Sivakumar, V. and Manthiramoorthy, S. 1991a. Individual and Combined Effects of Heavy Metals on Survival and Biochemistry of *Oreochromis Mossambicus. Indian J. Fisheries.* 38 (1) : 49-54.

James, R., Sivakumar, V., Sampath. K. and Rajendran, P. 1991b. Individual and Combined Effects of Zinc, Cadmium and Copper on Growth of *Oreochromis Mossambicus. Indian J. Fisheries.* 38 (3): 198-200.

Jhingran, V.G. 1991. *Fish and Fisheries oj India.* Hindustan Publishing Corporation. New Delhi, India.

Johansson-Sjobeck, M.L. and Larsson. A. 1978. The Effect of Cd on the Haematology and on the Activity of Delta-amino Levulinic Acid Dehydratase (ALA-D) in Blood and Haemopoetic Tissues of the Flounder, *Pleuronectes Americanus. Environ. Res.* 17: 191-204.

Kaviraj, A. 1989. Heavy Metal Concentrations of Fish and Prawn Collected from *Hooghly Estuary. Sci. Cult.* 55 : 257.

Kaviraj, A. and Konar, S.K. 1983. Lethal Effects of Mixtures óf Mercury, Chromium and Cadmium on Fish. *Environ. Ecol. 1 :* 153-158.

Khanna, S.S. and Gill. T.S. 1975. Effect of Cobalt Salts on the Glycemia and Islet Histology of *Channa Punctatus* (Bloch). *Acta. Anat.* 92 : 194.

Kumar A. 2002. Ecology of Polluted Waters. Vol.- 1. A P H Publishing Corporation, New Delhi, pp. 667.

Kumar, S. and Pant, S.C. 1981. Histopathological Effects of Acutely Toxic Levels of Copper and Zinc on Gills, Liver and Kidney of *Puntius Conchonius* (Ham.). *Indian J. Exp. Biol.* 19:191-194.

Mittal, V. 2004. Studies on the Toxic Effects of Some Heavy Metals in Freshwater Fish C. Mrigala. PhD Thesis, Department of Zoology and Aquaculture, CCS HAU, Hisar.

Mukhopadhyay, M.K., Ghosh. B.B. and Bagchi. M.M. 1994. Toxicity of Heavy Metals to Fish, Prawn and Fish Food Organisms of Hoogly Estuarine System. *Geobios.* 21 : 13-17.

Munshi, J.S.D. and Hughes. G.M. 1992. Air Breathing Fishes of India: Their Structure, Function and Life History. Oxford and IBH Publishing Co. Pvt. Ltd.. New Delhi, pp. 222.

Pandey, R.K., Arya, R.K., Verma, A. and Misra, S.K. 2004. Distribution of Heavy Metals in the Waste Water of River Pandu at Kanpur. *Poll. Res.* 23 (2): 335-342.

Ram. R.N. and Sathyanesan. A.G. 1983. Effect of Mercuric Chloride on the Reproductive Cycle of the Teleostan fish *Channa Punctatus. Bull. Environ. Contam. Toxicol.* 30: 24-27.

Rema, L.P. and Philip, B. 1996. Metallothiolein on Metallothionein Like Proteins and Heavy Metals Toxicity in *Oreochromis Mossambicus* (Peters). *Indian J. Exptl. Biol.* 34 : 527-530.

Sarkar, S.K. 1989. Evaluation of Two Heavy Metals on the Oxygen Consumption of *Tilapia Mossambica* (Peters). *Geobios.* 16: 108-110.

Sastry, K.V. and Subhadra. 1982. Effect of Cadmium on Some Aspects of Carbohydrate Metabolism in a Freshwater Cat Fish. *Heteropneuslcs Fossilis. Toxicol. Lett.* 14 : 45-55,.

Sehgal. R. and Saxena, A.B.N. 1986. Studies on the Toxicities of Cadmium and Zinc to a Freshwater Teleost *Puntus Ticto. J. Hydrobiol.* 2 : 33-35.

Sen, P.R. and Chatterjee, O.K. 1979. In Advances in Aquaculture, Edited by TVR Pillary and W.M.A. Dill (FAQ, England).

Sharma, M. 2003. Study of Biochemical and Histological Alterations Due to Some Aquatic Pollutants in Freshwater Fish *C. Mrigala.* M.Sc. Thesis, Department of Zoology and Aquaculture, CCS HAU, Hisar.

Shelly V. 2006. Effect of Heavy Metals on Histological and Biochemical Changes in Cyprinus Earpio and Cirrhinus Mrigal. Ph. D. Thesis, Deptt. Zool and Aqua., C C S Haryana Agri. Univ., Hisar, Haryana., pp. 37 + xxxiii.

Shelly V., Jain K.L. and Sabhlok V.P., 2006. Glycogen Reserves in Liver and Muscle Tissues of Freshwater Fish, Cyprinus Earpio L., as a Result of Heavy Metal Exposure. Bull. Environ. Contam. Toxicol. (In Press)

Sultana, R. and Rao, D.P. 1998. Bioaccumulation Pattern of Zinc, Copper, Lead and Cadmium in Grey Mullet, *Mugil Cephalus* (L), from Harbour Waters of Vishakhapatnam, India. *Bull. Environ. Contam. Toxicol.* 60 : 949-955.

Svobodova, Z. Zlabek. V. Celechovska. O and Janouskova, D. 2002. Metal Content in Tissues of Marketable Common Carp and in Bottom Sediments of Selected Ponds of South and West Bohemia. *Czech. J. Anim. Sci.* 47(8): 339-350.

Takeuchi,T. 1968. In: Pathology of Minamata Diseases: Study Group of Minamata Diseases. Japan. 11: 141.

Zhou, X.W., Zhu, G.N. and Sun, J.H. 2003. Effects of the Interaction of Heavy Metals on the Accumulation of Copper in the Tissues the Fish *(Carassus Auratns). J. Zhejiang-Univ. - Agric. Life Sci.* 28 (4) : 427-430.

GLOSSARY

Adult Stem Cell : Any stem cell taken from mature tissue, regardless of the age of the donor.

Autologous Transplant : Transplant using tissue from the same individual, or a twin.

Allogeneic Transplant : Transplant using tissue from a donor individual not genetically identical to the recipient.

Autoimmune Diseases : A constellation of different diseases all characterised by the failure of the body to distinguish "self" from "non-self" causing the body to attack its own tissues.

Blastocyst : A preimplantation embryo of 30-150 cells.

Cell Lines : Cultures of disaggregated tissue that can be maintained and propagated for use in research. The length of time cells will survive in culture varies. Some cell lines are *immortalised;* that is, they can be maintained essentially indefinitely, for one of a variety of reasons. embryonic stem-cells and embryonic germ cells are immortal because they express telomerase, one of the factors necessary for cells to propagate normally.

Chimera : An individual, organ, or part of an organism consisting of tissues of diverse genetic constitution.

Clinical Trial : Research to test the safety and efficacy of new treatments or to compare the effects of different treatments in patients or healthy volunteers.

Cryopreservation : The process of freezing biological materials in such a way that they can be stored for long periods of time, then thawed for use.

Ectoderm : The outermost of the three primary layers of an embryo; produces the nervous system, the epidermis and epidermal derivatives, and the lining of various body cavities such as the mouth.

Ectopic Tissues : Tissue that has formed abnormally temporarlly or spatially.

EG Cells : Embryonic germ cells. These cells are found in a specific part of the embryo/fetus called the gonadal ridge, and normally develop into mature gametes.

Embryo : Organisms in the early stages of growth and development. In animals, embryos are characterised by the cleavage of the fertilised eggs to many cells, the laying down of the three germ layers, and formative steps in organ development. Although there is some discussion about the characteristics marking the switch from embryo to fetus, in human beings, "embryo" generally refers to the time from implantation to about eight to twelve weeks after conception.

Endoderm : One of the three primary layers of an embryo; it is the source of the digestive tract and other internal organs.

Eukaryotic : Organisms composed of cells that have a nucleus *(i.e.,* the nucleus, where the genetic material resides, is separated from the rest of the cell, called the cytoplasm, by a complex membrane called the nuclear envelope).

Fetus : Organisms in later stages of development. In human beings, approximately eight to twelve weeks after conception.

Gamete : General term describing sperm and eggs.

Gene Therapy : The use of genetic material, usually DNA, to correct inherited or accumulated genetic damage.

Genome : The complete genetic code for individual or species.

Germ Cells : Cells comprising actual reproductive components of an organism (specifically, eggs and sperm, and their precursors).

Hematopoietic Stem Cell : Refers to a particular kind of stem cell that can restore blood.

In vitro : Refers to processes taking place in test tubes or similar containers.

In vivo : Refers to processes taking place in an organism.

Mesoderm : One of the three primary layers of an embryo; produces muscle, bone, and other related tissues.

Mesenchymal Stem Cell : A particular kind of stem cell that may give rise to tissues of mesodermal origin, including muscle, bone, and related tissues.

Monoclonal Antibodies : Antibodies produced in the laboratory by specialised cells called hybridomas. The important features of these antibodies include their specificity of binding to a single antigen (protein), the ability to produce them in unlimited amounts, and their homogeneity. These antibodies have proven to be very useful in the detection of several diseases (including, but not limited to, cancer and various viral infections) and in therapy (for certain cancers).

Pluripotent : Referring to cells able to give rise to virtually any tissue type, but not to a functioning organism.

Primordial Germline Cells : The source of embryonic germ cells. In normal development, these are the cells that give rise to eggs or sperm.

Recombinant DNA : Molecules that are constructed outside living cells by joining natural or synthetic DNA segments in such a way that they can replicate in a living cell (the replicative products are also considered to be recombinant DNA).

Somatic Cells : Refers to cells of the body excluding germ (reproductive) cells.

Stem Cell : In general, a cell with the capacity to reproduce itself, and to produce distinct differentiated tissue.

Trophoblast : The outer layer of cells of the mammalian blastocyst that gives rise to the placenta.

Totipotent : Refers to cells able to give rise to virtually any tissue type and, in some cases, as shown experimentally in mice, to a functioning organism.

Index